A HISTORY OF ENGLAND
IN A NUTSHELL

A HISTORY OF ENGLAND
IN A NUTSHELL

John Mathew

ATHENA PRESS
LONDON

A History of England in a Nutshell
Copyright © John Mathew 2007

ISBN 10-digit 1 84401 867 9
ISBN 13-digit 978 1 84401 867 3

First Published 2007 by
ATHENA PRESS
Queen's House, 2 Holly Road
Twickenham TW1 4EG
United Kingdom

Printed for Athena Press

For Laura and Emily so that they may acquire some knowledge of English history as well as Australian.

Contents

Preface

The interesting thing about history is that it all really happened, but in the end it is, as Gibbon wrote, 'little more than a register of the crimes, follies and misfortunes of mankind'. This is my summary of that register, which I hope will give young readers a concise overall picture of the first two thousand years of our Island's history, enable them to make use of it as a ready reference, and encourage them to read more widely so that they may appreciate that man's inhumanity to man merely demonstrates his overall desire to achieve a life of peaceful co-existence for which he continues to strive.

Introduction

The British Isles were once part of the continent we now know as Europe; the English Channel did not exist and a large part of the North Sea was land. At the end of the ice age (about 10,000 BC), when the vast area of ice in the north started to melt, the long process began which resulted in the island of Britain becoming separated from the European mainland and ultimately taking the geographical and physical shape which it has today. Since about the year 5000 BC, when Britain was sparsely populated with a few stone age hunters, this has probably seen little significant change.

In about 4000 BC, tribes from the continent began to arrive. Primitive farming started and stone buildings ('henges') were erected as places to worship their heathen gods. Stonehenge, the remains of which still exist to this day near Salisbury, is the most famous of these and is an incredible feat of construction. It is apparently related to a cult which worshipped the sun and was built between 2500 BC and 2000 BC, comprising an outer bank and ditch with eighty great blue stones transported over one hundred miles from south Wales and erected, some with lintels, in a double circle in the centre.

From about 1000 BC the Celts, one of the ancient peoples of western and central Europe, began to infiltrate Britain's shores. Tall and fair, they invaded in force in about 200 BC and, although the inhabitants of Britain opposed them, they seized most of southern England. It is probably from their Brythonic tribe that the name Britain is derived. They were devoted to superstitious rites and human

1

sacrifices, and their priests were known as druids. It was the druids who taught that mistletoe was sacred and holy and they would hang it in their places of worship, a custom that has lasted to the present day.

By the time of the Romans' arrival in 55 BC, the inhabitants were therefore predominantly Celts, who had by now mixed with the natives, resulting in a tough heathen race known as Britons.

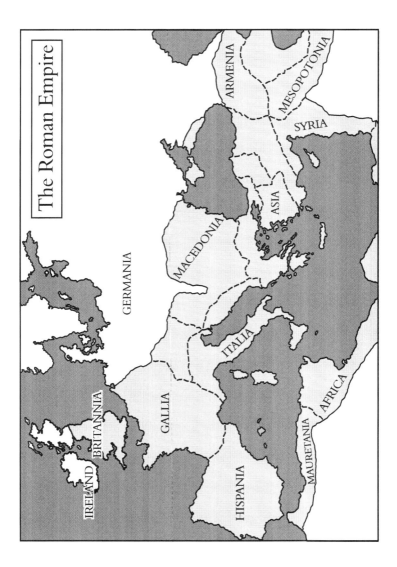

The Roman Empire

I

The First Millennium (55 BC–1066)

i   The Romans

The destiny of England really begins in 55 BC when Julius Caesar first landed on our shores.

By now Caesar had conquered Gaul and was looking for fresh conquests to maintain the authority and power of Rome. Virgil writes of 'Britain away from all the world', but word of the island across the sea from Gaul had been spread by traders who had sailed from the Mediterranean.

Caesar first invaded in the summer of 55 BC with about 12,000 men in eighty ships. Faced with the steep white cliffs of Dover and strong tides that were unknown in the Mediterranean, he decided to sail a few miles down the coast to the shelving beach where Deal now stands. Fierce fighting ensued but within a few days the Britons were negotiating for peace. As this first invasion was intended as a reconnaissance and Caesar had achieved his objective of understanding how to defeat the Britons and establish Roman rule, only nominal terms were imposed and the Romans retired to the mainland.

The following year, Caesar returned with a larger force. Resistance was strong, the Britons skilfully employing their chariots; but having been pushed back to the Thames at Wallingford they were again forced to negotiate a peace. With winter approaching and a revolt in Gaul, Caesar again retired to the mainland and later to Rome, where ten years later he would meet his death when stabbed by Brutus and his co-conspirators in the Senate House.

The second coming of the Romans was nearly one hundred years later when, in AD 43, the Emperor Claudius followed Caesar's example. This time, however, the Romans remained in Britain for the next 350 years.

Claudius's army was bitterly opposed by Caractacus, but he was eventually defeated by the Romans in south Wales and taken prisoner.

THE ROMAN EMPIRE

Following Caractacus' capture, the beautiful Boadicea, queen of the Iceni in East Anglia, then courageously led the opposition. Ultimately, in AD 62, she was defeated in battle by the Roman general Suetonius and poisoned herself rather than be taken prisoner.

The Romans then gradually took over the whole area we now call England. However the Welsh, the original natives who had been driven west, remained totally hostile, as did the warlike Scots, resulting in the building of Hadrian's Wall in AD 121 to protect England's frontier with Scotland. This great wall was named after the head of the Roman forces in Britain and substantial parts of it still exist between Carlisle and Newcastle.

Although at first the English were subdued by cruelty and massacre, subsequently the Romans settled peacefully and were responsible for sowing the first seeds of learning and culture.

A small settlement on the Thames was developed into a town, large by the standards of those days, which was called Londinium. Roman London covered an area of about one square mile on the north bank of the Thames, roughly between where Blackfriars and London Bridges now stand. The principle buildings were the amphitheatre, the forum, the governor's palace on the river front and the temple of Mithras (a Persian god). At that time the two main Roman religions were the worship of Mithras and Christianity.

Over the next 250 years the legacies left by the Romans included:

1) Their camps (*castra*) from which the words 'caster' and 'chester' are derived, e.g. Lancaster, Doncaster, Chichester and Manchester.

2) Roads, about 5,000 miles of them, tending to be straight and paved in stone, e.g. Watling Street from London to Chester and the Fosse Way from Lincoln to Exeter.

3) Buildings. The Romans knew how to erect large buildings from stone and brick. Surprisingly, after the Romans left at the end of the fifth century brick was not used again until 700 years later.

4) Christianity. This was first introduced into England by the Romans in the early fourth century AD after Constantine the Great became the first Christian emperor and converted the whole of the Roman Empire to Christianity.

In the middle of the fifth century the Roman army left England and returned to Italy to help protect their own country from the barbarian invasions. The Britons were now left without the protection of the Roman army and were ill-prepared to defend themselves from the continental invaders who were about to descend upon them.

The Roman occupation had been a peaceful one (*Pax Romana*), and brought order and prosperity to a previously fragmented and unruly country.

EASTER

It was Constantine who in AD 325 convened the Council of Nicaea to unify the early Christian Church. High on the agenda was to rule upon the date of Easter.

According to the New Testament, the resurrection of Jesus Christ took place on the first day of the week following Passover (a Jewish festival commemorating the release of the Israelites from Egyptian bondage). The first day of the Jewish week is Sunday and Passover starts on the day of the first full moon after the spring equinox. But as the spring equinox can fall on either on 20 or 21 March there was a good deal of confusion. The Council therefore ruled that Easter should fall on the first Sunday after the first full moon following the spring equinox, which itself was fixed for 21 March. Hence Easter is always a moveable feast.

Later it was discovered that the time taken for the earth to go around the sun was 365.25 days, and therefore a 'leap day' every four years in February was introduced to keep the calendar in balance.

Also in the sixth century the monk Dionysius Exiguus (Denis the Little) calculated the date of the birth of Christ and thus began the use of *Anno Domini* (AD).

The word 'Easter' probably comes from a pre-Christian festival held in honour of the Saxon dawn goddess Eostrae.

Easter eggs were originally hard-boiled hens' eggs. They were a forbidden food during the Lenten fast, but as the hens continued laying they were preserved by boiling, painted red to represent the blood of Christ and handed out as presents on Easter Day.

ii The Saxons

During the Roman occupation there had been regular raids from the tribes of northern Europe. Now they came in strength, the Angles and Saxons (who were a cruel tribe deriving their name from the use of a weapon, the *seax*, a short one-handed sword) from Germany, and the Jutes from Denmark (Jutland). Many of them settled in south and east England and pushed the Britons back from the coastal areas.

The two famous Saxon kings, and Horsa, landed in Kent in 449. A great battle took place on the river Medway at Aylesford in 455 and, although Horsa was killed, the Britons were defeated.

However, four centuries were to pass before Egbert, king of the West Saxons, became the first king of all England.

Over the 200 years between 450 and 650 the invaders gradually pushed the Britons to the far north-western corner of Britain, Strathclyde, and into Wales and west Wales (now Cornwall). The invaded area was thereafter called Angleland (England).

The German invaders were heathens, resulting in the expulsion of Christianity and it is from their gods that the English days of the week are named. The four principal Anglo-Saxon gods were Tu, Woden, Thor and Freia (hence Tuesday, Wednesday, Thursday and Friday). Sunday was the day of the sun, Monday the day of the moon, and Saturday was Saturn's day.

Around 500 a Roman-British leader was said to have held out in the west country, giving rise to the legend of King Arthur and the Knights of the Round Table, the greatest mystery of Saxon history. His deeds have been referred to by writers since the ninth century when the Welsh scholar Nennius recorded twelve great victories of this chivalrous warrior king against the barbarians. However, no proof of these deeds has ever been forthcoming; no one can say who he was, when he lived or if he even existed.

The Saxons, Angles and Jutes kept separate from each other and each included a number of small tribes, each with its own chief, rather than one great people. Hence the Angles inhabited Northumbria and middle Mercia, and East Anglia was divided into the North Folk (Norfolk) and the South Folk (Suffolk).

Saxon England

STRATHCLYDE

NORTHUMBRIA

MERCIA

EAST ANGLIA

WALES

ESSEX

KENT

SUSSEX

WESSEX

W. WALES

The Saxons went in all directions in the south: the South Saxons to Sussex, the West Saxons to Wessex (now Hampshire through to Devon), the Middle Saxons to Middlesex and the East Saxons to Essex.

Two tribes called Dorsaetas and Wiltsaetas settled in the areas now known as Dorset and Wiltshire.

Kent (named after the original tribe Centii) was another main Saxon area. The most important kingdoms were Northumbria (north of the Humber), Mercia in the midlands, and Wessex and Kent in the south.

The conversion of the Anglo-Saxons to Christianity really started after Gregory became pope and sent Augustine to England, who in 597 arrived at Ebbsfleet in Kent. At that time Ethelbert was king of Kent and his French wife Bertha was a Christian. Augustine was invited to stay with them at Canterbury, where he built a church. This was the first Canterbury Cathedral, a fairly primitive building but the only stone building in Kent at the time. Within a few years the people of Kent became Christians and the conversion of Northumbria and Mercia followed, helped by missionaries from Ireland who had recently been converted by St Patrick. Important Christian centres were set up in London and York, and Mellitus, bishop of London, built the first St Paul's Cathedral on the site of the old Roman temple of Mithras.

Celtic Christianity had existed before the arrival of Augustine, and was therefore in some ways different to the Christianity of Rome. In 664, at the Synod of Whitby, the bishops decided in favour of the Roman version.

In the year 800 Egbert became king of Wessex and he set out to make himself king of the whole country. He fought against, and won, the kingdoms of Kent, Essex and Sussex, and finally overcame Mercia and Northumbria.

In the south, the Britons (or Welsh as they were known, meaning 'foreigners') were driven further into Wales and Cornwall, where the river Tamar was fixed as their boundary.

By 827 Egbert became the first king of all England.

iii The Northmen

The Danes came not only from Denmark but also from Norway and were known as the Northmen or Vikings. At the end of the eighth century they started raiding the east coast of England in their longships and terrorised by pillage, rape and plunder. Soon they began to settle, building forts and marching against the English. In 851 they plundered London and many fierce battles took place. They might well have conquered all England had it not been for the accession of King Alfred in 871, grandson of Egbert, king of the West Saxons, and both a brave warrior and a great scholar. He had been taught by Swithin, the bishop of Winchester. (15 July is St Swithin's Day, and it is said that rain on that day will be followed by forty more, probably because of a great storm which took place when his relics were being transferred to Winchester Cathedral).

By the time of King Alfred's reign the Danes had conquered Mercia and marched against Wessex. After many battles, Alfred's soldiers eventually deserted him and he was forced to take refuge in disguise in Somerset, working for a shepherd. It was while he was living with the shepherd in his small homestead that he allowed the cakes to burn, giving rise to the well-known legend. Little did the shepherd's wife, who berated him for his negligence, appreciate who he was.

Eventually, when the Danes advanced into Devonshire and were beaten, Alfred came out of hiding, marshalled the people of Wessex and defeated the Danes in the battle of

Uffington. This victory was commemorated by the figure of a great white horse in the chalk on a nearby hill, which can be seen to this day near Swindon. This battle led to the making of peace, the Danes being allowed to rule in the north and the English in the south.

It was an uneasy peace because fresh invaders continued to attack from the sea. However, Alfred decided to meet like with like, building ships and forming the first British navy. The Danes in their longboats could now be attacked and pursued at sea, and within a short time Alfred's fleet was master of the English Channel and England was protected. 'Britannia ruling the waves' has been this island's main protection ever since.

We have already noted that Alfred was not only a soldier but a scholar, and he is renowned for beginning the first History of England, the Anglo-Saxon Chronicle, which still exists and remains the primary historical source of later Anglo-Saxon times. He also drew up a code of laws, wrote books, and started a translation of the Bible.

He was truly 'Alfred the Great' and died in 899 at the age of fifty-two.

iv The Tenth-century English Kings

Between 901 and 1016 there were no less than eight different English kings to whom we can refer very briefly.

Edward the Elder (901–925), son of Alfred, together with his sister Ethelfreda, Queen of the Mercians, continued the fight against the Danes, pushing them further north beyond Lincoln and Derby to an unknown area known as 'Dane-lagh'.

Edward was succeeded by his son Althestan (925–940), who gained an overwhelming victory against the Danes and their allies the Welsh at the Battle of Brunaburgh (937).

The next twenty years saw three further kings: Edmund

(940–946), Eldred (946–955) and Edwy (955–959).

It was during this period that Dunstan rose to become a power in the land. At the age of eighteen he was made Abbot of Glastonbury and in the reign of King Eldred was made his counsellor, becoming extremely powerful under King Edgar (959–975) when he was appointed Archbishop of Canterbury.

When Edgar died he was first succeeded by Edward, his son by his first wife, but he was murdered shortly afterwards on the instructions of his second wife, who wanted the throne for her own son. It was thus that Ethelred the Unready became king of England in 979 and began a disastrous thirty-seven-year reign. 'Unready' did not mean that he was ill-prepared. *Unred* was an Anglo-Saxon word meaning 'without counsel' or 'indecisive'. One of his first foolish mistakes was to quarrel with Dunstan, who was forced to leave the king's court. It was at this moment that the Northmen struck again with great effect. Sweyn, king of the Danes, and Olaf, king of Norway, joined forces, sailed into the Thames and took London.

Ethelred's only reply was to offer to pay them large sums to go away. This was accepted and the *Danegeld* tax was instituted to raise the necessary money. Unfortunately, as was to be expected, the Danes kept returning for more and gradually took over the whole of England, causing Ethelred to flee his country. By 1013 Sweyn, king of Denmark, became the effective king of England until his death the following year.

v   Canute and Edward the Confessor

Ethelred died in 1016 and was succeeded by his son Edmund, a brave and resourceful soldier who gained the title 'Ironside'. He valiantly carried on the fight against the Danes who were now ruled by King Canute, son of Sweyn.

After many battles it was finally agreed to divide England between them.

However, within a few months Edmund died leaving two very young sons, and Canute became king of all England.

He was a good and fair king to the English and Danes alike and divided the country into four divisions, each under the supervision of a 'jarl' or earl (the origin of that title), one of whom was Earl Godwin.

A well-remembered legend is told of Canute: while on the beach at Bosham with his entourage one of Canute's courtiers sought to flatter him by suggesting that if he commanded the incoming tide to stop he would be obeyed. Canute was angered, demanded a chair on which to sit, and ordered the waves to stop. Needless to say they did not, and the king was carried to safety, rebuking those who had sought to suggest that he had supernatural powers.

Canute died aged forty in 1035 and for the next seven years the country was ruled by two of his sons, first by Harold (1035–1040) and then by Harthacanute (1040–1042).

Harthacanute left no sons, and the people were determined to have an English king once more. Their choice was Edward ('the Confessor') who was the second son of Ethelred and who had taken refuge in Normandy during the reign of King Canute. He was supported by Earl Godwin and at first all seemed to go well. But Edward had arrived with many of his Norman friends and had adopted their manners and customs. When the English nobles found that the power had passed from the Danes only to fall into that of the Normans, it was not long before two rival parties emerged: the Normans under the king and the English under Earl Godwin, who was by now a very powerful figure in the land.

The English people supported Godwin and Edward was

forced to accept him and grant him favours at his court. When Godwin died in 1052, Harold, his son, followed in his footsteps and became the most powerful personage under the king.

Edward was a weak king and a religious man who is perhaps best remembered for building the first Westminster Abbey ('the Church of St Peter') on Thorney Island in the Thames, made of stone with the massive pillars and rounded arches of the severe continental style. It was not until after his death that he received the title of 'the Confessor', meaning 'one who had suffered for his religion'.

vi The Norman Conquest

Edward the Confessor died in 1066 and Harold, Earl of Wessex, although not the true heir, claimed the throne and was chosen by the Assembly of Councillors to take it. Harold had scarcely ascended the throne before William of Normandy made a rival claim.

Who was William and upon what basis did he make his claim?

About 200 years before, the Northmen had not only landed in England, Scotland and Ireland, but also in France. Some had settled there and founded the Duchy of Normandy, the capital of which was Rouen, and which by this time had a powerful ruler, William Duke of Normandy. Two years before Edward's death Harold had been shipwrecked on the Normandy coast and had been persuaded to take a solemn oath to recognise that William had claim to the throne of England on the death of Edward, although it was in fact a very slight one based upon being his cousin.

When Harold ascended the throne, William was enraged and demanded fulfilment of his promise. When this was not forthcoming, William marshalled a huge fleet and an army of 60,000, made an ally of Harold's brother Tostig, who wanted the throne for himself, and invited one of the great chiefs of Norway, Harold Hardrada, to come over and join him with his army.

Harold Hardrada landed in the north and joined forces with Tostig. Together they marched on York. Harold was forced to leave the Channel area and hurry north, where he defeated the invaders at the Battle of Stamford Bridge. Both Hardrada and Tostig were killed.

Unfortunately, within a few days the Normans landed at Pevensey in Kent virtually unopposed, and marched the few miles to Hastings before Harold and his army could hurry south, covering 200 miles in seven days.

The Battle of Hastings is one of the most famous battles in British history. The English soldiers stood in a great circle round King Harold, beating back the Norman attacks. Eventually the Normans pretended to run away and the English broke ranks to follow them. Immediately the Norman horsemen attacked but the ring remained unbroken. William then ordered his archers to fire their arrows in the air to fall on the Englishmen's heads and one of the arrows struck Harold in the eye, mortally wounding him. The English army fled and the Normans were victorious. Battle Abbey commemorates this great victory which led to Norman rule for the next one hundred years.

The Norman Kings

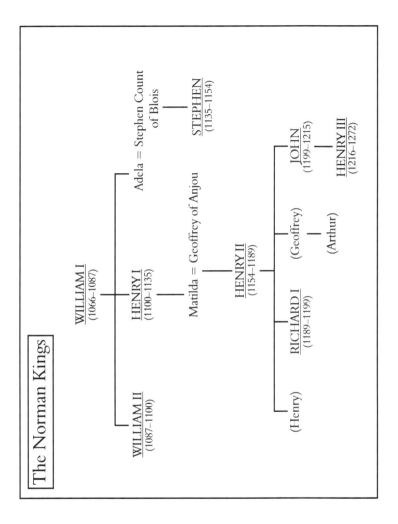

WILLIAM I
(1066–1087)

WILLIAM II
(1087–1100)

HENRY I
(1100–1135)

Adela = Stephen Count
of Blois

STEPHEN
(1135–1154)

Matilda = Geoffrey of Anjou

HENRY II
(1154–1189)

(Henry)

RICHARD I
(1189–1199)

(Geoffrey)

(Arthur)

JOHN
(1199–1215)

HENRY III
(1216–1272)

II

The Norman Kings (1066–1272)

i   William the Conqueror (1066–1087)

William the Conqueror had defeated the English at the battle of Hastings, but it was another five years before he could say he was master of all England.

In 1066, Britain was a divided country. The Saxons and Danes were maintaining an uneasy alliance, the Welsh (the original Britons who had been driven west by the Saxons) were permanently a potential thorn in the Saxon side, and the wild Scots in the north were ever ready to wage war across the border with England. Now the Normans had arrived, but when William was crowned king, the country became united against him and his barons.

The Normans spoke no English and William's arrogant and greedy barons compelled him to reward them for their services with grants of land and estates confiscated from their English owners. Hatred of the Normans was widespread and there were regular attacks upon them. It was this that caused the 'curfew' to be imposed. At sundown a bell would be rung and all English households had to extinguish their fires and remain in their houses overnight. The word 'curfew' is derived from the old French word *couvre-feu* meaning fire-cover.

One of William's English opponents was Hereward the Wake (meaning 'Awake') who now became a symbol of resistance to the hated Norman authority and who defied them for five years using guerrilla tactics. Ultimately

William came to terms with him and later defeated both the Welsh and the Scots.

By the early 1070s William had conquered the whole of England and he consolidated his insecure position by introducing the feudal system that had already been instituted successfully in Normandy.

When the king granted land to his barons he did so in return for certain services (paying 'homage'), the principal one of which was a duty to join the king with a certain number of men in time of war. The land that was granted was called the 'fief', the granter was the 'feudal lord' and the receiver was the 'Vassal'.

Sometimes the vassals of the king granted parts of their land to vassals of their own on the condition that they received similar services in return. In this way the king could always raise an army by calling on his vassals and they upon their under-vassals to rally to the royal command.

The feudal barons also administered local justice in their own manorial courts, while the king's sheriff did so in the shire courts, although the church courts were kept quite separate. At this time there was, of course, no common law and no parliament. The king ruled alone with the advice of his Great Council, made up of his chief feudal barons.

After the arrival of William the powerful English lords of the manors were replaced by foreign-speaking Norman barons, hated by their vassals because of the harsh and rigid feudal systems which were adopted.

William's reign is also remembered for the building of the Tower of London and the making of the Bayeux Tapestry, a huge embroidery of coloured wools stitched on linen. It was seventy-seven yards (seventy metres) long, although only twenty inches (fifty centimetres) high and depicted incidents from the Battle of Hastings to celebrate the Norman conquest. It was commissioned by the king's half-brother who was Bishop of Bayeux in

Normandy, although it was made in England.

The Domesday Book was another relic of William's reign. This was ordered by the king on Christmas day 1085 and recorded the results of a detailed survey of every village in the entire country. This enabled the king to keep himself informed as to the power of the barons and, more importantly, how much could be extracted from them in the form of taxes. It was presented to the king at old Sarum (present-day Salisbury) in August 1086.

The following year King William died from injuries received when he fell from his horse during the sacking of Mantes in France.

ii William II (1087–1100)

On the death of William the Conqueror, two of his ten children sought to be his successor. Robert, the eldest, was leader of the Norman barons in England, but William, a younger brother, hurried over from Normandy to claim the throne. The English rallied behind William because they hated the barons and he succeeded in taking the throne by force. In this manner, William Rufus ('the Red', due to his ruddy complexion) became king of England and duke of Normandy.

He was a physically strong and cruel man and a lover of hunting. As a result, he commandeered large tracts of land and forests for this pastime, forcing out the inhabitants and destroying their homes. One of the great forests he started was the New Forest (hence the name) in Hampshire, which stands in all its woodland beauty to this day.

Perhaps the Red King is best remembered for building Westminster Hall, now the gateway to the Houses of Parliament, one of the largest royal halls in Europe. It was large enough to hold three different courts for the judges and was rapidly to become the centre of the king's administration, including the Exchequer.

The Exchequer was a table covered by a black cloth marked into squares by white lines representing different sums of money. It has been described as 'a kind of abacus, a primitive manual computer on which the revenues and expenses of the kingdom could be reckoned and reviewed'. Twice every year, in the spring and autumn, the sheriffs of the counties would come to render their accounts. 240 silver pennies weighed one pound and, since the Normans called the English penny an *esterlin*, transcribed into Latin as *sterlingus*, the unit of account became known as the pound sterling.

When the sheriff paid over his taxes he would be given a tally, a hazel stick cut with notches to mark the amount he had paid. To provide each party with a record, the stick would be split lengthways below the handle, the two pieces being known as the foil and counterfoil. The longer piece which included the handle was known as the stock. In this way, the twelfth century was responsible for the terms Exchequer, sterling, counterfoil and stock becoming part of the language of English finance.

iii Henry I (1100–1135)

On William's death, mysteriously shot through the heart by an arrow whilst hunting, although his elder brother Robert was still alive he was again thwarted in gaining the throne, which was seized by a younger brother, Henry.

Henry 'Beauclere' ('the scholar') ruled for thirty-five years and, by and large, his reign was a good one. It was at this time that the mixing of the English and Normans really began, encouraged by Henry who set an example by taking an English bride. She was Matilda, a niece of Prince Edgar Atheling, who had made war against William and the barons. Supported therefore by the English, Henry routed the barons when they revolted against him, following them to France where he defeated his brother Robert at the battle of Tenchebrai (1106).

Henry had a son called William, to whom he was devoted, and a daughter, named Matilda after her mother, who married Emperor Henry V of Germany.

In 1120, William was drowned in an accident at sea and his father was overcome with grief; it has been said that he never smiled again. Matilda now became heir to the throne. Soon afterwards Henry V of Germany died and she married Geoffrey, Count of Anjou. He was known as Plantagenet', a word taken from the Latin *Planta genista*, meaning 'the broom plant' because he was accustomed to wear a sprig of yellow broom in his helmet. Their son Henry was therefore known as Henry Plantagenet when he subsequently became King Henry II in 1154.

In France, the Salic Law prevented a woman succeeding to the French throne, but no such law prevailed in England. In the last years of Henry's reign there were constant quarrels in the royal family between the English supporters of Matilda, the true heir, and the French supporters of his nephew Stephen of Blois, who felt that the French law should be followed in England. But when Henry I died in 1135 it was Stephen who was to become king.

iv Stephen (1135–1154)

Stephen was a weak king and his reign was a turbulent and unhappy one in which the people of England suffered greatly. There was continuous fighting between the king's supporters and those of Matilda, the barons reacting with great cruelty and the island dissolved into confused civil war.

It was not until 1153 that an agreement was reached (The Treaty of Wallingford) under which Stephen was to remain king until his death, but that thereafter Matilda's son

Henry should become king. Thus did Henry become the first Plantagenet king when Stephen died in 1154.

v   Henry II (1154 – 1189)

Henry Plantagenet, married to Eleanor of Aquitaine, was a wise man of strong character and he successfully reigned for thirty-five years. He defeated the Scots and conquered Ireland but never succeeded in subjugating the Welsh; he ultimately made peace with them and left them to manage their own affairs.

He is particularly remembered for his reforms of the feudal system which diminished the power of the barons. Instead of military service he demanded money from them, thereby allowing him to pay for his own army made up of English freemen. He also made radical changes to the legal system, the King's Court (the *Curia Regis*) becoming a regular court staffed by lawyers and trained officials, and he appointed judges to form the first King's Bench. The assize system was also introduced whereby the judges travelled the country administering common justice in the major towns. He was therefore responsible for introducing the structure and procedures for the administration of justice and local government as we know it today.

Henry is also remembered for his relationship with Thomas Becket. Thomas was the son of a merchant from Rouen, but he was born and bred in London, and became Port Reeve (now the equivalent of Lord Mayor of London), Chancellor and finally Archbishop of Canterbury.

In the early 1170s Canterbury Cathedral, originally built by King Ethelbert and Augustine in about 600, was destroyed by fire. In 1174 the new Cathedral in the form we know it today rose from the ashes, designed by a Frenchman, William of Sens, based upon the cathedral he had built in the French town of that name.

Thomas Becket was a great favourite of the king, hence his rise to power and prominence, and he, like the king, lived in great style and luxury. The Church in England was by now becoming a very powerful force, embracing most of the educated men and owning lands and properties that made them very rich. When Thomas became archbishop, head of the Church, he sought to increase this power, with the result that his relationship with the king began to deteriorate and matters came to a head when they quarrelled over the jurisdiction of the judges.

Henry tried to improve the administration of justice by appointing judges to act fairly to all. But the Church maintained that all churchmen (that is, all those in any way connected with the Church) should be tried by the ecclesiastical courts presided over by a bishop, as was the custom throughout Europe, and Becket would not allow them to be tried by the Judges. Neither of them would give way on this issue.

Another bone of contention was whether the bishops and clergy, who owned great areas of land, should pay homage to the king as did the barons. Becket also refused to submit to this. In the end, Henry called a meeting of the barons at Clarendon in 1164 and the Constitutions of Clarendon were agreed, Henry's first piece of major legislation. Not only were the first statutory criminal offences thereby introduced but also other laws, including the jurisdiction of the king's courts over churchmen and paying of homage by the clergy.

Becket still refused to comply, was banished from the land and sought refuge in the town of Sens in Normandy. After six years Henry reluctantly allowed him to return to Canterbury, where thousands of people gathered to welcome him back. So angered was the king by the reception given to someone who had refused to obey him that he ranted against Becket and finally uttered those well-remembered words: 'Who will rid me of this turbulent priest?'

It is almost certain that he did not intend this hasty exhortation to be taken literally but four of his barons did and, under the leadership of Reginald Fitzurse, they plotted his death. On the evening of 29 December 1170 the four armed barons invaded the cathedral and found Becket in a small chapel with three loyal friends, where he was set upon and murdered. When Henry heard of Becket's death he displayed the most sincere remorse and did public penance before the tomb as atonement for his guilt. Becket was proclaimed a martyr and within two years was canonised.

The end of Henry's reign is marked by his defeat at Le Mans in France by his enemies, who had been joined by his two sons Richard and John. This defeat and the treachery of his sons led to him dying an unhappy death in 1189. His deathbed was attended by only one illegitimate son to whom Henry is alleged to have declared: 'But it is the other ones who are the real bastards!'

vi   Richard I, Cour de Lion (1189–1199)

Henry II left two sons, Richard and John, who both became kings of England. They were very different in character and each is remembered for very different reasons.

Richard the Lionheart ruled for ten years, most of which was spent out of the country fighting in the Crusades in the Holy Land or protecting his possessions in Normandy. He was a sportsman and a soldier of great strength and bravery, although his subjects were to pay heavily for his adventures. He loved war but 'the advantages gained by his military genius were thrown away through diplomatic ineptitude'.

For over a century the Turks, who were Moslems and worshipped Mohamed, had been attacking the Holy Land, a Christian country which we now know as Palestine and the capital of which was the holy city of Jerusalem where Christ was crucified. During this period the Catholic countries of Europe had been sending armies to protect the Holy Land and oust the Turkish invaders. These wars were known as the Crusades or 'Cross-ades': wars on behalf of the Cross.

Two great crusading orders in England had headquarters in London: the Knights of St John at Smithfield who organised the medical services and the Knights Templar in the area which became known as the Temple and which now houses two of the Inns of Court, Middle and Inner Temple.

When Richard came to the throne of England the Turks were in control of Jerusalem and he was eager to take part in defeating them in order to support both the cause of Christianity, as well as to indulge his spirit of adventure and his love of fighting. To raise the necessary funds he sold most of his realm, including the selling of every office of state, the avoidance of military service by payment of scutage, and the sale of Roxburgh and Berwick to the king of Scotland for 10,000 silver marks.

The stories of his deeds in Palestine make exciting reading and are well recorded.

When returning in 1192 he was shipwrecked and forced to travel through a region of Austria controlled by the Archduke Leopold with whom he had quarrelled. Richard was captured, imprisoned and sold to the Holy Roman Emperor Henry VI, who demanded as ransom the staggering sum of 150,000 marks, twice the annual revenue of England. However, the State and the Church were 'under the feudal obligation to ransom the Liege Lord, above all when he enjoyed the sanctity of a crusader'. The money was therefore raised, nearly bankrupting the country. It has been recorded that Prince John, who was to be the next king, 'set an example by collecting these taxes throughout his shires. His agents dwelt upon the sacred duty of all to pay but he kept the proceeds of their faith and loyalty for himself.' Richard finally returned home in March 1194.

However, it was not long before he was off to the wars again, this time against King Phillip of France, in order to protect his possessions in Normandy. It was to be his last campaign as the need to finance it led to his death in 1199. Treasure was alleged to have been found buried in land belonging to the Lord of Chaluz who resisted the king's claim to it. The king laid siege to the castle of Chaluz and as he rode near the wall he was struck in the shoulder by a bolt from a crossbow and died later from the wound. The manner of his violent death reflected the manner of his violent lifestyle. Robin Hood, the outlaw of Sherwood Forest, is supposed to have lived during his reign.

vii John (1199–1215)

On Richard's death, John managed to seize the throne by cruelty and subterfuge and became the most detested of English kings.

Henry II had four sons. Henry, the eldest, had died childless. Richard I was now dead and likewise had no children. The third son, Geoffrey, was also dead but had a eleven-year-old son, Arthur, who was the rightful heir to the throne. But John, the fourth son, a cruel and selfish man, was determined to become king himself and he and his supporters seized and imprisoned his nephew. Arthur was subsequently murdered, allegedly slain by John's own hand. In this unhappy way John gained the throne, becoming a hated monarch who made enemies on all sides. He refused to obey the religious orders of the church, he took vast sums from the barons and nobles and tried to seize their land and he robbed the poor unmercifully to fill the royal coffers. It is not surprising, therefore, that the people of England united against him and, led by the barons, forced the king to accede to their demands, which were enshrined in Magna Carta.

All important documents were at this time written in Latin, since it was the common language of those few Europeans who could read and write. Magna Carta is the Latin for 'The Great Charter'.

In 1215 the barons, for once supported by the people, met at Brackley in Northamptonshire, their number including Stephen Langton, one of the most famous archbishops of Canterbury. A message was sent to the king threatening to make war upon him and depose him unless he promised no longer to break the law and overlook the people's rights. The king was furious, but when he appreciated that effectively the whole of the country was about to rally against him and he was in no position to resist, he agreed to meet the barons at Runnymede on the River Thames near Windsor. It was here on 15 June 1215 that the Great Charter was sealed by the king and the barons.

It contained forty-nine articles setting out the laws and customs which the king was required to keep but, having been drafted by the barons and the clergy, it was to a large extent a selfish class measure designed to perpetuate the privileges of the aristocrats and the church rather than those of the common people.

Many of the articles were very relevant at the time but have no such relevance today; others however still affect British life. This applies particularly in regard to the administration of justice. Here are some examples:

- Article 40: 'To none will we sell, to none will we refuse, to none will we delay, Right and Justice.' For nearly 800 years this has remained the foundation of our judicial system in that everyone is entitled to the same justice without undue delay, a justice which cannot be bought.

- Article 17: Provided for the Court of Common Pleas to sit in a fixed place rather than to follow the king's court in its travels. Initially this place was the Palace of Westminster and there it remained until the end of the nineteenth century when the Royal Courts of Justice were opened in the Strand.

- Article 18: Provided for two of the king's judges to visit each county four times a year to dispense justice in the principal town. One of the judges heard criminal cases (the 'Red Judge', because he wore a red gown) and the other (the 'Black Judge') dealt with the civil disputes. This reorganisation of the assize system started by Henry II remains much the same to this very day.

- Finally, trial by a jury of one's peers was enshrined in the administration of criminal justice by Article 39.

It will therefore be readily appreciated that Magna Carta was one of the most significant milestones in British history and it is mainly for this reason that King John is remembered. The will of the people was imposed on a despotic king and the foundation of freedom and democracy was established.

Nevertheless it had little immediate constitutional effect. What the barons really wanted was to rid themselves of the king and they invited Louis, son of the French king Philip, to bring troops to England and with their assistance to seize the Crown. In the result, the last year of John's reign was a year of civil war, the anti-royalists being assisted by the French until John died of dysentery in October 1216 and the justification for the revolt died with him

viii Henry III (1216–1272)

King John was succeeded by his nine-year-old son, Henry, who reigned for fifty-six years. It was a reign of misery and unrest for the people of England and is perhaps best remembered for the rebuilding of Westminster Abbey as it is known today, and for Simon de Montfort and the first English Parliament.

Henry married a French woman, Eleanor of Provence, and her foreign friends came over to England in large numbers to be given castles and lands and to be made bishops and archbishops by her indulgent husband. They were despised and hated, which led to an opposition party, not of English barons but a nationalist party, being formed under the leadership of Simon de Montfort, Earl of Leicester, a brave and honourable man. Quarrels soon broke out with the king, who was now breaking the promises made by his father in Magna Carta.

At this time, the government of the country was in the hands of the king and the ministers whom he appointed. Simon de Montfort took the same course against Henry as the barons had done a few years earlier against his father, King John: he took up arms against him and defeated him at the Battle of Lewis in 1264. Not only was the king then made to promise to keep the charter but also to agree to a council to advise him and to decide the fair amount of money to be paid by the barons and the people for the running of the country.

The First Parliament was therefore called in 1265. It consisted of twenty-three barons, and 120 churchmen and representatives from the counties ('Knights of the Shire') and from the towns ('Burghesses'). It did not sit for very long and was largely ineffectual but it was the beginning of the democratic Parliamentary system which remains in place today.

Simon de Montfort had many enemies and later that year Henry, together with his son Edward, felt strong enough to challenge him once more. De Montfort was defeated and killed in the Battle of Evesham (1265) and the royal authority was restored.

Henry died seven years later and was buried in his beloved Westminster Abbey, thus ending a long reign that did little for the good of the English people.

It was during this period that Roger Bacon, the famous Franciscan friar, first taught and experimented with various scientific projects including the making and use of gunpowder.

III

The English Kings (1272–1485)

i   Edward I (1272–1307)

It has been mentioned that the Saxons had slowly driven the Britons west to Cornwall and Wales. By now Cornwall had become part of England, and the Saxons and Britons who had settled there had successfully integrated. But the Welsh had never submitted, and indeed had become more powerful than ever before under the leadership of Prince Llewellyn, and border fighting constantly took place.

Edward I, a wise king and experienced soldier, resolved to change that situation and, having raised a large army, marched into Wales. Many battles were fought and ultimately, in 1282, Llewellyn was killed in battle and Edward became master of the Welsh, building castles to secure his new principality.

However, he was a wise conqueror and allowed the Welsh to keep their language and customs and to be governed separately, although they were made to accept English laws. Edward's young son was made the first Prince of Wales in 1301, a title bestowed upon the English monarch's eldest son ever since.

From this time the history of Wales as a separate country came to an end, although it took another 200 years before Wales was united with England and had representation in Parliament.

Edward then turned his attention to Scotland. The Saxons had originally spread as far north as the Lowlands and by now Scotland was divided among many different clans, little kingdoms in themselves, over whom the Scottish kings had no unified power.

When Alexander III, king of Scotland, died in 1285 and his granddaughter Margaret ('the Fair Maid of Norway'), daughter of King Olaf, died on her way to become queen, John Balliol emerged as king from many other claimants including Robert Bruce.

Edward now decided that the time was ripe to become master of Scotland as he had of Wales, so he headed his army north and captured Berwick-on-Tweed, which was then a Scottish town. It has remained part of England ever since but was the only part of Scotland that he succeeded in taking. Edward gained other victories, including the battle of Falkirk (1298), and reached Scone where the famous Stone, upon which the kings of Scotland were crowned, was seized and removed to Westminster Abbey, where it remained until 1996.

These defeats and humiliations united the divided Scots under William Wallace and they fought back under his leadership until he was taken prisoner and executed in 1305.

By 1307 Edward had still not conquered Scotland but he continued trying to achieve this end until his death in Cumberland as he was preparing to cross the border for a final determined assault. His death probably saved Scotland because his son, who succeeded him, was as weak as Edward had been strong and was as unfit a ruler as his father had been outstanding.

We cannot leave this reign without recording the fact that in 1290 Edward expelled the Jews from England. During the previous century bad feeling towards the Jews had been steadily growing, both on religious grounds and because they were money lenders. They had been systematically ruined as a result of Henry III heavily fining them to raise much needed revenue and by now had largely been replaced as financiers by Italians. They were now expendable, so Edward cancelled all remaining debts and pleased the pope by expelling the entire Jewish community.

Also in 1290 Edward's wife, Eleanor of Castile, died in Nottingham. It had been a marriage of love and not the usual arranged marriage of political convenience. Her body was brought to London for burial and everywhere the cortège stopped Edward built crosses. The last stopping place was in London at Charing (an Anglo-Saxon word for 'turning') where the road turned to Westminster and Charing Cross was erected.

Edward's death came at the end of one of the great centuries in British history, one which saw the evolution of Parliament, the foundation of the universities and Inns of Court, the building of great cathedrals and castles and the beginnings of a fairer society.

ii Edward II (1307–1327)

This was a twenty-year reign of defeat and mismanagement, during which the Scots finally defeated the English and maintained their independence for the next 300 years.

After the capture and death of William Wallace, Robert the Bruce, who was the son of the Robert Bruce who had lost his claim to the throne to Balliol twenty years before, took over command of the Scottish army.

Edward II had withdrawn his army from the borders when his father died, and had no stomach to continue the fight for supremacy in Scotland. The English soldiers in Scotland were left to fare for themselves while Edward quarrelled with his barons in the south.

This gave Robert the Bruce a free hand and his army recaptured many Scottish towns from the English until the only fortress left in English hands was Stirling Castle. When Bruce marched on Sterling, King Edward was compelled to try to save it and raised a huge army of 100,000 men which met a much smaller army of the Scots at Bannockburn on 24 June 1314. But the English army was routed by Bruce's superior tactics. Robert Bruce became king of Scotland and all hopes of a unified England and Scotland were lost.

When Edward ascended the throne he was already obsessed by a young handsome Gascon called Piers Gaveston and he now lavished riches and power upon him, making him 'Keeper of the Realm' (effectively ruler of England) when he went to France to marry Isabella, the daughter of Philip IV. Thereafter, it was said that Edward loved Gaveston more than his queen and the barons, who hated the young favourite, rose against the king and forced Gaveston's banishment. He was ultimately seized and murdered in 1312.

A reforming middle party under the Earl of Pembroke began to emerge and Edward in reply sought to build up a royalist party headed by the Dispensers, a father and son both called Hugh. Young Hugh Dispenser subsequently became the object of the king's affections and so disgusted his wife Isabella that she became the lover of Roger Mortimer, one of the Welsh Marcher Lords who had fled to France. In 1324 the Dispensers tried to annul Isabella's marriage to the king and were responsible for her estates being sequestrated. Isabella and Mortimer had been planning to depose Edward in order to enable her son, Prince Edward, to accede to the throne and they now returned to England at the head of a small army of exiles. The unpopular king had little support and Isabella's revenge was swift and complete: the Dispensers were both hanged in 1326 and the miserable Edward imprisoned and cruelly murdered in Berkeley Castle the following year, ending a most unhappy and ignominious reign.

iii Edward III (1327–1377)

When Edward III was crowned in 1327 he was fourteen years of age and his mother Isabella and her lover Mortimer seized the reins of power, effectively ruling England for the next three years. They were deeply unpopular, as they represented only a minority of the nobility, conceded English interests in France and abandoned all claims to Scotland by recognising Robert the Bruce as king. In 1330 Mortimer was kidnapped, accused of the murder in Berkeley Castle and hanged. Isabella was thereafter kept in permanent captivity by her son who, now aged eighteen, assumed the royal responsibilities.

The new king was an extrovert and adventurer and was popular, having a loyal and loving wife, Isabella, who bore him fourteen children. His reign was particularly significant for his military successes and the start of the Hundred Years' War against France. One of the excuses for this war was the French support given to the Scots, England having resumed its quarrel with Scotland. Further, the lucrative wool trade to the Low Countries was in danger due to disruptions placed on the trade by the aristocracy of Flanders who held French sympathies, and the merchants on both sides of the Channel were clamouring for England to take action.

Such a war required exceptional funds which, in the circumstances and in a time of prosperity, Parliament was prepared to vote. The Commons was now beginning to sit in the Chapter House of Westminster Abbey separate from the barons, and the splitting of the Houses of Parliament into the Lords and the Commons dates from this time.

Edward landed in The Hague with an army of 30,000, getting less support from the Belgians than expected. He was confronted by a powerful French army of 120,000 at the village of Crecy, where, on 26 August 1346, the famous

English victory took place. This was a battle memorable for the effect of the English archers equipped with long bows, for the bravery of the king's sixteen-year-old son the Black Prince and for the fact that gunpowder was used in battle for the first time to fire a small, but largely ineffectual, cannon.

This great victory no doubt encouraged Edward to continue the war. The English achieved other victories, notably the capture of Calais after a twelve-month siege (1347) and at Poitiers when John, king of France, was taken prisoner (1356). Nevertheless, it was largely a pointless war. Great areas of France were ruined and England's territorial gains were short-lived. The war was still in progress when Edward died in the fiftieth year of his reign.

He was by then a widower, his wife having died from the plague eight years before, and he was suffering from senile dementia. But England mourned the passing of this chivalrous warrior.

It was he who, on St George's Day in 1348, instituted the noble, chivalric Order of the Garter, his own Round Table of twelve of his closest knights, which was subsequently increased to twenty-five. St George had replaced Edward the Confessor as patron saint of England and their company was called that of St George of the Garter.

Why Garter? Legend has it that Edward was having an affair with the Countess of Salisbury who dropped her garter at a celebration ball after the fall of Calais. The king recovered it and placed it on his own leg to the sniggering of his courtiers who knew of the relationship. He rebuked them with the words *Honi soit qui mal y pense* ('evil be to him who evil thinks'). The garter became the symbol and this phrase became the motto of the new order. Incidentally, in 1945 Winston Churchill turned down the award after his defeat in the general election, saying, in typical Churchillian fashion, 'I can hardly accept the Order of the Garter from the king after the people have given me the Order of the Boot.'

iv   Richard II (1377–1399)

Edward III had seven sons including Edward the Black Prince, John of Gaunt (Gwent) who was Duke of Lancaster, Thomas Duke of Gloucester and Edmund Duke of York. His heir was his grandson, Richard, aged eleven, the son of the deceased Black Prince, who became king with his uncle, John of Gaunt, as Regent. It was not a happy reign and eventually in 1399 Richard was deposed, imprisoned and murdered.

One of the most important events which took place during the early part of this reign was Wat Tyler's Rebellion in 1387, when the king was fifteen years old. The people had been heavily taxed to pay for the wars against France and Scotland and now the unpopular poll tax was introduced, a tax of twelve pence on every person over the age of sixteen ('polle' meaning 'head'). This does not sound very much until is appreciated that at that time a labourer earned about one penny for a full day's work.

When the tax collector called on Walter the Tiler he not only demanded the tax but insulted Wat's daughter. In anger Wat struck and killed him and, when the news spread, it acted as a catalyst for the rising of the people in south-east England, with Wat Tyler at the head. They marched on London and by the time they reached Blackheath numbered over 100,000. They threatened to overthrow the government unless various concessions were made in regard to their living conditions. They actually succeeded in taking possession of the Tower of London and eventually the king agreed to meet their leaders in Smithfield ('smooth field').

The Lord Mayor of London, Sir William Walworth, who accompanied the king, lost his temper with Wat Tyler, drew his sword and killed him. The crowd was about to attack the royal entourage when the young king, with great courage, stepped forward and, by promising to meet their demands and be their leader in place of Wat Tyler, persuaded them to disperse. In this way a very dangerous rebellion was brought to an end, although the royal promises were never kept and later the other leaders were arrested and hanged.

The young King Richard now determined to take the reins of power into his own hands. John of Gaunt, who was an unpopular figure, was removed and ministers of the king's own choice were appointed, the chief of whom was Michael de la Pole, Earl of Suffolk. The king also strengthened his position by marrying Anne, daughter of Emperor Charles of Germany, in 1382.

But it was not long before a rival party was formed, hostile to the king and headed by the king's uncle Thomas Earl of Gloucester and Henry Bolingbroke, son of John of Gaunt. They accused the king's ministers of treason, forced the Earl of Suffolk to flee and retook positions of power.

In 1387 when the king came of age he again asserted his royal authority by dismissing Thomas and Bolingbroke. But it was not until ten years later, in 1397, that he was in a position to take full revenge by accusing them and their friends of plotting another rebellion. Thomas was imprisoned and killed and Bolingbroke was banished.

In 1394 King Richard, whose wife Anne had died, married Isabella, daughter of the French king, and temporarily brought peace between England and France. In 1399 he headed an expedition to Ireland where his rule was threatened by an armed rebellion and while he was away Henry Bolingbroke saw his opportunity to regain power, returning and rallying his friends and followers. The king hurried back from Ireland but was too late to save the day. He was forced to abdicate, imprisoned in Pontefract Castle and starved to death. In this manner Henry Bolingbroke gained the throne as Henry IV.

Richard II's reign will also be remembered for two other famous people. Geoffrey Chaucer (born in 1340) became the first great English poet and wrote the *Canterbury Tales*. By now the French language of the rich and upper classes was becoming mixed with the Anglo-Saxon English of the middle and lower classes, and the English language as we know it today started to evolve. Chaucer was one of the first writers to use this language which enables us today to read and understand the tales in their original form.

The other well-known person was the ill-tempered John Wycliffe (1321–1384) who denounced the pope and preached against the superstitious dogma of the church and the corruption and dissolute living of many of the clergy. He translated the Bible to support his teaching and attracted many followers called 'Lollards' (a Dutch word meaning 'a mumbler of prayers').

Finally, one cannot leave the fourteenth century without mentioning the Black Death, the terrible plague that came to England from the continent in 1348 and spread across the country, rising and falling over the next twenty-five years. The effects were horrendous and resulted in the death of millions, and the population was probably more than halved. Sneezing was an early symptom of the disease and the scent of flowers was thought to give protection from the germs, hence the ghoulish origin of the nursery rhyme:

> 'Ring a ring o' roses
> A pocket full of posies
> Atishoo, atishoo, we all fall down.'

It returned again in a less virulent form in 1360 and 1369 when it claimed the life of Philippa, the devoted wife of Edward III, among others.

v   Henry IV (1399–1413)

For the next fifty years or so England was ruled by the three Henrys of the House of Lancaster, starting with Henry Bolingbroke, Henry IV.

Henry's position was precarious because he was not the true heir to the throne. He had achieved it by force and persuaded Parliament to support him, thereby rendering himself dependent on that support and therefore under an obligation to Parliament, who used it to increase their powers. The true heir was Edmund Mortimer, Earl of March, great-grandson of Edward III.

It was a reign of continuous strife. Henry was never free from the fear of civil war and within months of his coronation he successfully put down the first uprising against him. This was followed by a more serious rebellion in Wales led by Owen Glendower and at the same time by the Scots who rose on behalf of King Richard who they maintained was still alive. In 1402 the Scots were defeated by the Earl of Northumberland at the battle of Homildon Hill.

Northumberland then quarrelled with the king and joined Glendower in Wales in support of Edmund Mortimer. In 1403 they were comprehensively defeated by the king at Shrewsbury.

In the meantime, the French attacked and captured Jersey and Guernsey, sacked Plymouth and landed in the Isle of Wight. However, the Scots' threat was diminished by the capture of James, heir to the crown of Scotland, on a ship on his way to France.

Northumberland, who had been defeated at Shrewsbury, again marshalled an army and again was defeated at Bramham Moor (1408), being killed in the battle, and the Welsh were further defeated in 1409 despite assistance from the French.

But just as it looked as if Henry had finally overcome his enemies, he contracted leprosy, from which he died in 1413.

He was succeeded by his eldest son, Henry V.

It was during this reign that the Lollards were officially declared heretics and the infamous statute, De heretico Comburendo, was passed in 1401 which legalised the burning of heretics at the stake and led to the widespread killing of Lollards. The pope even ordered that Wycliffe's bones should be dug up (he had died twenty years before) and burned.

vi Henry V (1413–1422)

Henry V was brave, successful and admired by his people, becoming their hero with his incredible victory over the French at Agincourt.

At an early stage Henry decided that the only way to end the civil wars that had marked his father's reign was to turn his people against a foreign enemy. He therefore claimed the French crown, raised a small army and invaded France. On 25 October 1415 (St Crispin's Day), the two armies met in battle near the castle of Agincourt. The English army, exhausted and ill-supplied, numbered about 15,000, while the French army was probably over three times as large.

The English victory, in which half the French were killed or taken prisoner, was emphatic and stunned the whole of Europe. The chapel at All Souls College, Oxford, is a memorial to this great battle.

A second successful campaign further strengthened Henry's position in France and in 1420 he married Catherine, daughter of the French king Charles VI, on the promise that he would succeed to the French throne on Charles' death. But shortly afterwards war broke out again and during Henry's third campaign in August 1422 he fell sick and died.

His widow Catherine later married Owen Tudor and

their grandson was later to become Henry VII, the first of the Tudor kings.

Thereafter, following the succession of Henry V's young son who grew into a weak and ineffectual monarch, the English power in France steadily declined.

vii Henry VI (1422–1461)

Only Calais and the Channel Islands remained in control of the English. His son, Henry VI, was just nine months old when crowned king of England with his mother's bracelet on his tiny head. The power was then held in the hands of three regents: the Dukes of Bedford and Gloucester and Henry Beaufort, Bishop of Winchester.

Joan of Arc was the unlikely saviour of France. A teenage peasant girl from Domrémy, she dreamt that an angel had told her that she would take part in bringing happier times to France. She therefore sought out the dauphin, who was so impressed with her fervour that he sent her to join the French army which was then trying to raise the siege of Orléans. Riding on her white horse in armour, the soldiers were so moved by her bravery and leadership that the siege was soon raised, beginning the decline of the fortresses of the English in France. In 1430, still only eighteen years old, she was betrayed to the English and burned as a witch in the marketplace in Rouen.

The failures of the English in France continued after the death of Joan, Paris falling in 1436 and Maine abandoned in 1444. The young king then married Margaret of Anjou, a strong and formidable lady, but peace was short-lived and five years later, when war broke out again, the English lost Normandy. In 1453 Bordeaux was retaken by the French and only the town of Calais then remained in English hands.

The Hundred Years' War which had begun in the reign of Edward III was over but a thirty-year war in England was destined to follow, the Wars of the Roses. For this reason it is difficult to say precisely when Henry V's reign ended.

He was the founder of Eton College and King's College, Cambridge.

viii The Wars of The Roses (1455–1485)

Henry VI was descended from John of Gaunt, Duke of Lancaster, son of Edward III.

Richard, Duke of York, was descended from Edward III's youngest son, Edmund.

Both, therefore, had a claim to the throne but it was not until Henry had reigned for over thirty years that civil war broke out between the houses of Lancaster and York, each side supported by some of the great noble families of England with the Earl of Warwick, the most powerful subject in the country, supporting York.

By 1453 King Henry's weak mind had virtually rendered him ineffectual, although his wife Margaret remained a strong and powerful personality as queen. Henry's reign had so far been one of ceaseless war in France but now the French possessions had been lost and what remained of the returning army was only too ready to serve any leader who promised fighting and plunder.

The emblems of the two sides were the red rose of Lancaster and the White Rose of York. The origin of this dated back to a quarrel that took place in the gardens of the Temple church on a summer's day in 1451. Richard, Duke of York, and the Earl of Somerset, of the House of Lancaster, were walking in the Gardens with friends when a quarrel arose and sides were taken. Somerset plucked a red rose from a bush saying, 'Let those who are with me wear my flower.' Then York took a white rose and said the same. Hence the cruel and bloody conflict which followed became known as the Wars of the Roses.

The war started in 1455 when the party of York won a victory at St Albans. Somerset was killed and the mad King Henry taken prisoner. Battle after battle followed, the ascendancy of each house see-sawed and, as each party gained the upper hand, their captured opponents were mercilessly slaughtered. At Wakefield, in 1460, the Duke of York himself was captured and murdered. The following year, however, the Yorkists triumphed at Towton when 60,000 men were killed shortly after the Duke of York's son, Edward, had been proclaimed king with the support of the Earl of Warwick ('Warwick the Kingmaker'). Henry fled to Scotland and Edward now reigned as King Edward IV of England.

It was not long before Edward offended Warwick over his marriage to Elizabeth Woodville, who was a Lancastrian of no great rank, causing Warwick to change sides. He now supported Henry and set out to remove Edward.

Edward was entrapped and captured by a party of Lancastrians but escaped. Two further battles later took place in the spring of 1461 at Barnet when Warwick was killed and Tewkesbury when King Henry was captured and beheaded and the House of York was completely victorious. Edward was now undisputed as king of England and reigned for the next twelve years but, as we shall see, the Wars of the Roses did not finally end until fourteen years later when Richard III was defeated and killed on Bosworth Field.

ix   Edward IV (1461–1483)

As already mentioned, Edward was first proclaimed king in 1461 after the Yorkist victory at Towton, his father Richard Duke of York having been killed at Wakefield the year before. However, he was not undisputed king until the final defeat of the Lancastrians at Tewkesbury in 1461, which was followed by the murder of King Henry in the Tower. Edward's reign then continued for another twelve years and, although he was an undistinguished monarch, he was undoubtedly popular and this period saw the beginning of the growth of wealth in England through trade and the emergence of a class of rich merchants. The civil war had been responsible for the deaths of many of the nobility of England and their estates and riches were now seized by the Crown, making Edward no longer dependent on Parliament for money.

Unfortunately, bitterness and hatred still existed between the houses of York and Lancaster and, in 1478, Edward put to death his own brother, the Duke of Clarence (allegedly by drowning in a vat of wine) convinced that he was plotting against him. In 1483 Edward died leaving two young sons, Edward and Richard, aged twelve and nine, destined to be murdered by Edward IV's younger brother Richard, Duke of Gloucester, in order to seize the crown as Richard III.

x   Edward V and Richard III (1483–1485)

After Edward IV's death, he was succeeded by his eldest son Edward, aged twelve, with his uncle, Duke of Gloucester, as regent. But Gloucester immediately asserted that Edward was illegitimate and persuaded Parliament to crown himself king as Richard III. Edward and his younger brother were imprisoned in the Tower ('the Princes in the Tower') and were smothered as they lay in their beds, no doubt to prevent any rally to their cause. But Richard came to be attacked from other directions and his reign lasted only two years before he was killed by his enemies in battle. It came about in the following way.

It will be remembered that Henry V's widow Catherine

had married the Welshman Owen Tudor and there was a grandson, Henry Tudor Earl of Richmond, who was a Lancastrian. It was to him that the Lancastrians now looked as their champion. Both sides marshalled their forces which met at the famous battle of Bosworth Field, near Leicester on 22 August 1485. Both Henry and Richard fought with great courage but when part of Richard's forces under Lord Stanley deserted to Henry's side, the tide began to turn against the king. He led attack after attack in his efforts to kill Henry of Richmond but, in the end, he lost his horse and became the last English king to die in battle. The well-known quotation from Shakespeare's *Richard III* records this moment: 'A horse! A horse! My kingdom for a horse!' The headgear that he had worn into battle was recovered from under a bush and was used then and there symbolically to crown Henry VII on the field of battle.

So fell Richard of Gloucester, the last of the Plantagenet kings, and so commenced the period of the Tudors. Henry VII married Elizabeth, a daughter of Edward IV and the Wars of the Roses finally ended, the reconciliation of Lancaster and York symbolised by the red and white rose of the House of Tudor.

Richard has been recorded as a cruel and evil man. Maybe he was, although there are some distinguished historians who challenge this opinion and cast doubt on his complicity in the murders of the Princes in the Tower. Shakespeare depicts him as an evil and deformed hunchback but it should be remembered that most contemporary accounts of his reign were written by his enemies. However there is little doubt that he attained the throne by subterfuge and violence and few appear to have mourned his death.

We cannot leave this period of history without mentioning William Caxton who introduced the art of printing into England in 1477. Caxton was a successful wool merchant living in Bruges, the centre of the European wool market, who amused himself by translating a long French poem 'The Tales of Troy' into English. He was asked for copies and, rather than labour to do so in manuscript, he went to investigate the new printing process then being started by Dutch printers in Bruges. He was so impressed that before long he had his own press and in 1477 returned to England where he set up the first printing press in London. Printing brought about a revolutionary change in England and, indeed, the world, because it introduced more widespread availability of knowledge and learning to everyone.

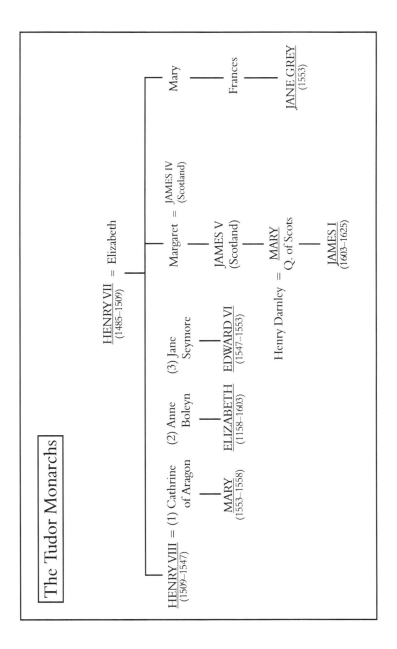

The Tudor Monarchs

HENRY VII = Elizabeth
(1485–1509)

HENRY VIII = (1) Cathrine   (2) Anne   (3) Jane
(1509–1547)   of Aragon   Boleyn   Seymore

Margaret = JAMES IV
(Scotland)

Mary

MARY   ELIZABETH   EDWARD VI
(1553–1558)   (1158–1603)   (1547–1553)

JAMES V
(Scotland)

Frances

Henry Darnley = MARY
Q. of Scots

JANE GREY
(1553)

JAMES I
(1603–1625)

IV

The Tudors (1485–1603)

i   Henry VII (1485–1509)

The Tudor period lasted 118 years. Henry VII was the first of the Tudor sovereigns, being followed by Henry VIII, Edward VI, Mary and Elizabeth I.

Although the House of Lancaster had won the day at Bosworth Field and Richard was dead, there were other princes of the House of York who had a better right to the crown than Henry, and so he was preoccupied with the uncertainty of his own position. Edward IV had a daughter, Elizabeth, in addition to his sons, Princes Edward and Richard, who had been murdered in the Tower. Henry, in a wise effort to secure his position and unite the Houses of Lancaster and York, married her in the first year of his reign. Nevertheless there were two serious rebellions against him.

The first was that of Lambert Simnel, the young son of an Oxford carpenter, who was used by the Yorkist Lord Deputy of Ireland, the Earl of Kildower, to impersonate the Earl of Warwick. Warwick was a nephew of Edward IV and his father was the Duke of Clarence who had been drowned in the vat of wine. An obvious contender for the crown, Henry had shut him up in the Tower and kept him there. It was now pretended that he had escaped and that Lambert Simnel was that very person, so that he could be used to persuade friends of the House of York to take up his cause against Henry. A large number of Yorkists did so and Margaret of Burgundy, Edward IV's sister, sent over a small army of trained soldiers to help. Henry took immediate action. He had the true Earl of Warwick taken from the Tower and paraded through the streets of London and sent an army to meet this insurrection. In 1487 Henry won the battle of Stoke when Simnel was taken prisoner and thereafter forced to work as a scullion in the royal kitchen.

The second rebellion was that of Perkin Warbeck five years later. This time it was Prince Richard, Duke of York, who was impersonated on the basis that he had not been smothered in the Tower but had escaped and taken refuge abroad. Again Margaret of Burgundy lent her support and so also did the Scots. Perkin Warbeck landed in Cornwall, but although some Cornishmen joined him, Exeter closed its gates to him and he was finally defeated by the king's army at Taunton.

The town of Exeter was rewarded by King Henry with the gift of a sword which can be seen in Exeter Guildhall today. Henry spent a large part of his reign trying to keep out of war with the three great powers on the continent: France, Spain and the Empire (now consisting of Germany, Austria and the Netherlands). By and large he was successful and he was equally successful in raising revenue for other causes so that he soon became far richer than any previous king of England.

He achieved this in a number of ways. It had become the custom for retainers and friends to wear the livery of the noble whom they followed. Henry now forbade this custom and heavily fined those who continued it. He also collected large sums by way of 'Benevolences', meaning things given voluntarily and not under compulsion. In fact it was a form of blackmail because those invited to give knew full well that if they refused they would soon be compelled to do so.

To get over the difficulty of those who disputed his right to make them pay, Henry set up the Court of Star Chamber, the judges of which were generally his friends.

Artist unknown, *King Henry VII*, 1505, National Portrait Gallery, London.

It was a dangerous precedent because it was independent of the common law and came to be hated because those who appeared before it did not receive a fair trial. It was later ended by Parliament and kings of England were forbidden to ever set up such a court again.

Some of the revenue that was raised was used by Henry to establish what was effectively the first 'standing army' that England ever had. Because he felt that both his life and his throne were constantly threatened, he arranged for a permanent bodyguard to attend and protect him wherever he went. They were called the Yeomen of the Guard.

King Henry had four children: Arthur, Margaret, Henry and Mary. He married Margaret to James IV, king of Scotland, and although this did not immediately affect the enmity between the two countries it ultimately had that desired effect. Their son James had a daughter, Mary, who became Queen of Scots and it was her son, James VI of Scotland who afterwards became James I, king of England and Scotland.

He also married his elder son Arthur to Catherine of Aragon, daughter of the king of Spain, and, when Arthur died, persuaded the pope to allow his younger son Henry (later Henry VIII) to take his brother's widow as his bride.

Henry's reign saw the discovery of America by Christopher Columbus and when he died in 1509 the Yorkist problems were over, England was peaceful and united and the state treasury was overflowing.

ii Henry VIII (1509–1547)

We now come to the story of Henry VIII and his long reign. Fond of sport, fond of good living, he was also fond of having his own way and was selfish, vindictive and overbearing. But, whatever his faults, to the day of his death he was beloved by far the greater number of his people. We know what he looked like because Hans Holbein, one of the greatest portrait painters, began painting in England during his reign and left us some famous pictures of him. He was considered dignified and handsome, although we might have thought him overweight and somewhat florid. Some of the greatest men of the time were his ministers, but when they disagreed with the king they discovered a man stronger than themselves, a man who was dangerous to oppose.

Henry came to the throne when he was eighteen and reigned for thirty-eight years at a time when great changes were taking place in England. During that period he married no less than six times. As we shall see, his reign witnessed some momentous events that resulted in far-reaching changes to the social and religious structure of the country. As already mentioned, in the early sixteenth century there were three great powers in Europe: France, Spain and the Empire, all of which considered that England ranked below them. At the beginning of his reign Henry was the friend and ally of Spain because he had married King Ferdinand's daughter, Catherine of Aragon, and this automatically made him the enemy of King Louis XII of France. In 1513 there was a short war with France which led to an overwhelming victory for Henry at the Battle of the Spurs (so-called because the French cavalry panicked and fled on their horses). Relations with France therefore deteriorated further and this enmity resulted in a more important battle between the English and the Scots, the battle of Flodden Field.

How was it that the battle of Flodden sprang from the quarrel between Henry and Louis XII? It came about in this way.

Artist unknown, King Henry VIII, 1505, National Portrait Gallery, London.

In 1513, while Henry was with his army defeating the French, James IV, King of Scotland and an ally of France, picked a quarrel with England and ordered Henry to leave France. Henry, needless to say, refused and James therefore invaded at the head of a large army of 100,000, crossing the Tweed and camping on the side of Flodden Hill in front of the river Till. The Earl of Surrey hurriedly called the northern counties to arms and advanced to Flodden with an army of less than 25,000. It was a famous victory for the English, who were foolishly allowed to cross the Till and take up positions which were difficult to attack. King James was killed and Scottish casualties were high, but the English did not follow up the victory, being content that Scotland was no longer in a position to help the French. However, this turned out to be of little consequence as peace was made between England and France the following year. At that time, though friendships were quickly broken, they were also quickly re-established. As a condition of peace Henry gave his sixteen-year-old beautiful sister, Mary Tudor, as a bride to the old king of France. Happily for her, Louis lived only a very short time thereafter and Mary at once married the Duke of Suffolk, whom she had always loved.

It was during this time of wars and treaties, promises made and promises broken, that a great man rose to fame in England: Thomas Wolsey. Son of a wool merchant, educated at Oxford, he entered the church and became employed by Henry VIII. But it was not until Henry VIII became king that Wolsey began to rise rapidly to become the wealthiest and most powerful man in England. The most agreeable of companions and the wisest of counsellors, he became Cardinal, Papal Legate and Lord Chancellor, accumulating power that has probably never been equalled in England since. Stories are told of his wealth and the style of his living in the splendid palace he built at Hampton

Court. But he was also a man of arrogance, the object of great envy and, importantly and unhappily, he was not content with his achievements because there was a bigger prize to be won: he had set his heart on becoming pope. It was an ambition which was to bring about his downfall and alter the course of English history.

As already mentioned, Henry had married his brother's widow, Catherine of Aragon, daughter of the king and queen of Spain. Henry and Catherine had one daughter, Mary (later to become queen), but no son. This caused Henry discontent because he longed for a male heir to the throne. He had also grown tired of his wife and wanted to marry Anne Boleyn, one of her ladies-in-waiting, but in those days divorce was impossible except by leave of the pope. So Wolsey was dispatched to Rome to persuade the pope to give consent upon the excuse that it had been unlawful for Henry to marry his brother's widow, despite the fact that the pope had given his consent for the first marriage. However, Wolsey found himself faced with a very difficult situation. The pope, Clement VII, was at that time in fear of Emperor Charles, who was exerting military pressure on him. Now Charles was the nephew of Queen Catherine and was determined to prevent his aunt being discarded by Henry in favour of another woman. But not only did the pope want to avoid offending Emperor Charles, but Wolsey, hoping to become pope himself, did not want to offend Clement. The result was that pope Clement refused to sanction a divorce and Wolsey failed in his errand.

Henry was furious, blamed Wolsey and from that moment withdrew his favour from the Cardinal and set about causing his downfall and ruin. In October 1529 Wolsey was removed as Lord Chancellor and, although he sought to retrieve his position by giving his wealth and estates to the king, Henry showed no mercy. In November

1530 Wolsey was arrested and charged with treason but, broken in health and spirit, he died before he could be executed.

Wolsey's failure to obtain papal consent did not make Henry any the less determined to get rid of his wife and marry Anne Boleyn. Until this time, Henry had always accepted the power of the pope and supported him as the only true head of the church. In the end, the pope declared that the king of England should henceforth be known as the 'Defender of the Faith'. In the light of what happened thereafter it is a very strange title for the monarchs of England to have kept till the present day, as witnessed by the letters F.D. (Fidei Defensor'), which still can be seen on British coins.

Henry now began to consider whether, after all, a king of England was bound to obey the pope and whether it would not be possible to declare, once and for all, that the king of England was not bound to obey any foreigner. It was at this moment that two men came forward to tell him just what he wanted to hear: that it was his duty to do exactly what he wanted to do.

These two men were Thomas Cranmer and Thomas Cromwell, the latter of whom had been secretary to Cardinal Wolsey. Both were quickly rewarded. Cranmer was made a bishop and two years later Archbishop of Canterbury and Cromwell became the king's most trusted minister.

For some years a new movement had been growing in Europe, particularly in Germany and the Netherlands (as Holland and Belgium used to be called). This movement was known as the Protestant Reformation and was headed by a German monk, Martin Luther, who began to attack the pope and the church. The pope had always forbidden the Bible to be freely translated, only allowing it to be printed in Greek or Latin. This was one of Luther's complaints together with many others, including the selling of 'indulgences', which was the widespread practice of paying money for the (pretended) forgiveness of sins. Luther's objections or 'protests' led to his followers being called Protestants and a fierce struggle began between the Protestants and the Roman Catholics, which overflowed into England and led to the Reformation and the ultimate establishment of the Protestant Church of England.

Also, at this time, an era of 'New Learning' was taking place in England. This was led by Erasmus, Thomas More and Colet, and was helped by the advent of printing which made literature available to the reading public, allowing them to think for themselves and to find out many things that their priests had never told them. Erasmus was a Dutch monk who taught in England, Thomas More a lawyer who became Speaker of the House of Commons and Lord Chancellor, and John Colet a great scholar who became Dean of St Paul's and founded the famous London school of that name. They denounced the ignorance, worldliness and greed of the monks and higher clergy, and it was therefore the abuses rather than the doctrine of the church that they attacked.

The Protestant Reformation and 'New Learning' became the allies of Henry, who had no wish to fight alone against the pope since his power was great both in England and on the continent. What could be more natural than that Henry should become friends with the pope's opponents? Henry accepted the Protestant leaders into England and allowed the Bible to be translated into English and read in the churches. He also made Thomas More Lord Chancellor. But in order to get his own way he went further and declared himself head of the Church of England, persuaded Cranmer to declare Catherine to be divorced and married Anne Boleyn.

Pope Clement was very angry and excommunicated him, but there was no stopping Henry now he had set out on this course. Henry demanded that everyone admit that he alone was head of the church and imprisoned those who refused, confiscating their property. Unhappily, some of the noblest men in England were among his victims, including Sir Thomas More, Lord Chancellor. The good and worthy More was one of the king's best friends and though he was ready to serve and obey Henry, he was not prepared to do what he believed was wrong. He certainly did not believe that the king had any right to disobey the pope and therefore refused to accept him as head of the church. He was thrown into the Tower, convicted of treason and executed.

The irony of the situation was that Anne Boleyn, over whom Henry had quarrelled with the pope, was later alleged to have been unfaithful to him and on 19 May 1536 was also executed in the Tower. She left one child, Elizabeth, who was destined to become the famous queen of England. The day after Anne's execution, Henry married Jane Seymour, one of her ladies-in-waiting.

Although Anne Boleyn was dead, Henry's quarrel with the pope continued. The church owned a large part of the country and many valuable estates which housed the monasteries and nunneries. Many of the clergy led dissolute lives and were a disgrace to their church, and Henry used this as an excuse to take the great wealth they possessed. Thomas Cromwell was largely responsible for suppressing the monasteries, hundreds of which were broken up and destroyed and, in transferring their wealth to the king and to a new nobility, gave them a vested interest in supporting this Reformation. But not everyone was prepared to accept the changes and rebellions broke out in Lincolnshire and Yorkshire, which had to be subdued.

A year into her marriage to Henry, Jane Seymour gave birth to a son, Prince Edward, and died a few days later. He was proclaimed Prince of Wales and later was to become King Edward VI. Two years later Henry married again, this time to a German princess, Anne of Cleves. She was said to be very beautiful but in fact was exceedingly plain and could speak no English. The marriage was never consummated and within a short time Henry decided to get rid of her, venting his anger on Cromwell, who had many enemies with accusations to which the king was now prepared to listen. Cromwell was arrested in 1540, tried for treason and executed. Henry then divorced Anne of Cleves who was treated kindly and lived in comfort for many years. Henry immediately married his fifth wife, Catherine Howard, an attractive and tempestuous twenty-year-old who was not content with a husband thirty years older than herself and who, within two years of marriage, suffered the same fate as Anne Boleyn when a reckless love affair was revealed. In 1543, eighteen months later, the king married his sixth and last wife, Catherine Parr, who was fortunate enough to outlive her husband.

Henry had always considered that one of his responsibilities was to foster the notion of bringing England, Scotland, Ireland and Wales into some form of peaceful coexistence. Towards the end of his reign he had put down Lord Fitzgerald's revolt in Ireland and had taken the title of King of Ireland (1542). The following year he achieved unity with Wales and the Act for the Government of Wales was passed which meant that Wales was now under English law. From that date Welsh representatives have sat in Parliament. But Scotland remained a thorn in his side, particularly as the Scots were allies of the French, and another war broke out in 1542 when James V of Scotland headed his army in another invasion but was defeated.

In that same year, on 7 December, Mary, daughter of James of Scotland, was born and only seven days later her father died. Mary therefore became queen: Mary Queen of Scots. Henry, in an attempt to secure the succession to the English throne on Prince Edward and to achieve unity between England and Scotland, proposed his young son's betrothal to the infant Queen of Scots. But this was not acceptable to the northerners and a further war ensued, also involving France. This position of confrontation still remained when Henry died in 1547. His reign was momentous in many ways but particularly because of his break with Rome, his six wives and his ruthless use of power.

iii   Edward VI (1547–1553)

Edward VI was only nine years old when he ascended the throne. He was, as already mentioned, Henry VIII's only son, by Jane Seymour who had died shortly after his birth, although Henry also had two daughters, Mary, daughter of Catherine of Aragon and Elizabeth, daughter of Anne Boleyn.

But the law of England gave sons the right to succeed before daughters. The Seymour family was Protestant and Jane's brother Edward Seymour, Earl of Hertford, persuaded the king's council to appoint him Lord Protector of the young king and to bestow the title of Duke of Somerset upon him. The king had been brought up as a Protestant and Somerset, with Cranmer's help, now 'proceeded to transform the political reformation of Henry VIII into a religious revolution'. The bishops who would not accept the king as head of the Church of England were removed and replaced by Protestants, and a new prayer book, written in English, was compulsorily introduced in all the churches. Under Somerset the reformed church effectively took the place of the Roman Catholic Church in England, but troubles lay ahead.

England at this time was facing the worst of economic crises. The population was increasing, there was widespread unemployment and Henry's debasement of the currency had led to massive price increases. This led to the seizure and enclosure of common land by a corrupt and greedy nobility and the breaking up of monasteries meant that the accustomed charity from the monks was no longer forthcoming. Discontent was rife throughout the land and there were uprisings against land enclosure, particularly in East Anglia and the West Country. John Dudley, the Earl of Warwick, suppressed these rebels and assumed the leadership of the opposition to the hated Somerset. He persuaded the king to make him Duke of Northumberland and, with other powerful friends, accused Somerset of treason, bringing about his trial and execution in early 1552.

Northumberland now became Lord President of the Council and a most powerful person, effectively ruling the country through the boy king, who had the poorest health and was expected to die in the very near future. Northumberland therefore set about securing his position of power. He married his son to Lady Jane Grey, a great-grandniece of Henry VIII and then persuaded the dying king to disinherit Henry VIII's daughters, Mary and Elizabeth, in favour of Lady Jane.

Edward VI died on 6 July 1553 when still only fifteen years old. His reign was a short but important one because it witnessed a major step in the Reformation that finally led to the creation of the Church of England as it is known today. It must be remembered that Henry VIII had no sympathy with those who wanted to change the Catholic doctrine. His disagreement with Rome was basically in regard to the authority of the pope over the church in England. He wanted to have that authority for himself, a desire that stemmed from his wish to be divorced from his first wife, Catherine of Aragon. From this time the new religion of Martin Luther in Germany (whose followers were called Protestants or Reformers) began to infiltrate England. The difference between them and the Catholic followers of the pope was whether the way in which the Christian religion was taught by Rome was the right way or not. The pope claimed the right to say how the church should be governed in England (and, indeed, in other European countries) and maintained that those who belonged in any way to the church were under the laws of the church and that the king's courts had no jurisdiction over them. He also said that no bishop could be appointed except by him and that he could punish those with whom he quarrelled. The Reformers now said the pope could no longer be the Head of the church in England and ought to have no power to punish Englishmen for what they did, said or thought.

But there was a more important difference than this. The pope claimed that there was only one true form of the Christian religion and that was the form taught by the bishops and priests under the authority of the pope, and that they were the only persons to interpret the true meaning of the Bible and to decide what was right and wrong. The Protestants, on the other hand, maintained that any man should be allowed to think and judge for himself with the help of the Bible, prayer and his conscience. To this end they wanted the Bible and services in the churches to be in English, instead of Latin which few were able to understand.

The struggle had been started by Henry VIII for selfish reasons. It continued under Edward VI, who sought to establish the reformed church, and now Queen Mary was to appear on the scene to fight back for Catholic convictions.

But, as we have already noted, under the influence of Northumberland, Edward VI had decreed that it was Lady Jane Grey who should succeed him.

iv Lady Jane Grey

The sad reign of Lady Jane Grey was so short that her name is not listed in the monarchs of England and she tends to be forgotten. She was only seventeen, reigned for just nine days, and within a year had been deposed and executed. She was good, charming and highly educated but was used by others for their own ends and died for their crimes and causes.

On the death of King Edward, two major parties grappled for power: the Protestants, led by Northumberland, and the Catholics who were determined that Mary, daughter of Henry VIII and Catherine of Aragon, should become queen. Northumberland prevailed upon the council to declare that the rightful heir to the throne was his daughter-in-law, Lady Jane and Mary fled to friends in a strongly guarded house in Suffolk, fearing she would be imprisoned. Her fears were justified, but when Northumberland, for whom the people had no love, set out to attack her, support for Mary came from all sides and Northumberland's cause was lost. He was apprehended, sent to the Tower and executed.

Lady Jane and her husband were also imprisoned in the Tower and at first it seemed that their lives would be spared. They might well have been had it not been for a serious Protestant uprising in Kent led by Sir Thomas Wyatt in support of Jane, which led to Mary and her advisors deeming her too much of a danger to be allowed to live. Charming all who met her, even her gaolers, she died the bravest of deaths on the scaffold.

v Mary I (1553–1558)

Mary was an inflexible woman of thirty-seven when she came to the throne, determined to save England from the heresy of the new religion and to return the people to the church of Rome. On both sides there were men and women who believed that the religion to which they belonged was the only true one and that those who did not agree should be punished for the good of the country and for the sake of the true religion. They were prepared to give up their lives for what they believed and to take the lives of those who disagreed with them. If a referendum could have been taken, the people of England might have voted for a half-way house, a Catholic country independent of Rome. But they did not have that choice as Mary was determined to restore Catholicism with full allegiance to the pope, her single ambition being reunion with Rome.

Mary was the first queen of England to reign in her own right. She was unmarried, but resolved this situation in a most unfortunate way when, without advice, she took it upon herself to agree to marry Philip of Spain, son of Emperor Charles V, the greatest of Catholic monarchs. Being the daughter of Catherine of Aragon, Mary had an affinity with Spain not shared by the people of England, who regarded Spain as an enemy and had no wish to have a Spanish king of England. Mary married Philip on 25 July 1554, and though Parliament decreed he should have no power to interfere with the government of the country, there was a fear he would influence the queen, and from that moment her popularity declined.

It immediately became apparent that both the king and the queen were of one mind in putting down the Protestants. Parliament decreed that henceforth the pope was the only true head of the church and that anyone refusing to obey this new edict could be put to death. And so the persecutions commenced, earning the queen the title 'Bloody Mary'. Seven senior Protestant clergy were imprisoned, including Bishops Hooper, Latimer and Ridley, and Cranmer, Archbishop of Canterbury. Hundreds of men and women all over the country who refused to give up their beliefs and revert to Catholicism were imprisoned or put to death. No less than 300 were burned at the stake, including the three bishops mentioned above, and Latimer's last words to Ridley as the fire was lit turned out to be prophetic: 'We shall this day light such a candle by God's grace in England as, I trust, will never be extinguished.'

The following year, 1556, the same fate befell Cranmer. Tortured, humiliated and worn out by two years of imprisonment, he finally gave in and signed a document rejecting the Protestant faith and accepting the pope's authority. But this was not to save his life and at the stake he stood by his Protestant faith and denied the document in which he had recanted, holding out the hand which had signed it to be consumed first by the flames. They became known as the English Martyrs, immortalised by John Foxe's *Book of Martyrs* and the Martyr's Memorial in Oxford.

There is little doubt that Mary thought that what she was doing was right and that it was her duty as Queen and a Christian, but the people thought she was wrong and she became more disliked as every month went by. Many, who had cared little about the new religion, now began to move towards the faith of those who they had seen persecuted and had died so bravely. The Protestants themselves, instead of being frightened into changing to the old religion, now became determined to get rid of the Queen and her Spanish husband who believed that the Pope had a right to interfere with the lives of the people of England.

Mary was in love with her husband but he did not return that affection and was only too happy to return to Spain as king of that country when his father died in 1556. Mary's final humiliation came when Philip persuaded her to join in Spain's war against France which led to the loss of Calais, England's last stronghold on the Continent. Mary was overcome by this disgrace: 'When I die,' she said, 'you will find the word "Calais" engraved upon my heart.'

Deserted by her husband, disliked by her people, Mary was now a disillusioned and unhappy lady. The pope, who Mary had always done her best to serve, had sided with France against Spain and therefore had now become her enemy. She had become seriously ill and had no child to inherit the crown. The next heir to the throne was her sister Elizabeth, the daughter of Anne Boleyn, who she hated and who was the Protestants' favourite.

Mary died on 17 November 1558, unhappy and disappointed. Her reign was one of the most hateful and miserable in our history and few felt any sorrow on her death. The persecutions and cruelties perpetrated on her behalf means she will always be remembered as 'Bloody Mary', but few women have tried harder to do what they believed was right and it would be unfair to forget this when we read the story of her reign.

vi   Elizabeth (1558–1603)

Elizabeth was a remarkable woman and for the next forty-five years was to be a remarkable queen. She was twenty-five years old when she came to the throne, knowledgeable in history and philosophy, educated in French, Italian, Latin and Greek and a gifted musician and dancer. She remained good-looking and dignified until she died and from the time she became queen showed a caution and good judgement not to be expected in a woman of her age. Edward VI had tried to reign as king of the Protestants, Mary as queen of the Catholics, but Elizabeth sought to be queen of all the people of England whatever their faith and beliefs, although she was wise enough to declare herself on the side of the Reformers who were ready to support her.

She inherited a country in economic crisis and was faced with other difficulties as well. France and the Pope declared that she had no right to the throne and that the true heir was Mary Stuart, the Catholic Queen of Scotland, and even Spain, England's ally at that time, was against her succession for religious reasons. However the people of England welcomed her as queen and appeared to support her.

One of Elizabeth's first decisions was also one of the wisest. She appointed William Cecil to be her chief minister and he was to serve her faithfully for forty years, no sovereign ever having a better friend and adviser. He was created Lord Burleigh and rewarded with great power and riches.

Elizabeth herself held no strong religious convictions and, in order to resolve the urgent religious question, set upon an immediate course of compromise designed to unite as many of her people as possible. In 1559 the Act of Uniformity was passed which enacted that all church services should be of a uniform pattern and held in English and a modified Book of Common Prayer was introduced and made compulsory. This was acceptable to the majority but not to the extremists of both religions, the extreme Protestants, followers of the French preacher Calvin, being called Puritans. They believed that the Reformation had not gone far enough and that the Church set up under the Act of Uniformity was too much like the Roman Catholic Church and needed to be 'purified'. In order to carry out the Act a special court was set up, the Court of High Commission, which tried and punished Catholics and Puritans alike.

Also in 1559, the of Supremacy was passed which declared all persons to be guilty of treason who did not accept the Queen's title to the throne.

There was another important question, other than that of religion, which was a cause of concern to Elizabeth and her ministers at the beginning of her reign and that was the question of the Queen's marriage. This was important in order to assure a Protestant heir to the throne but it was also important politically that she married the right person. There was no lack of suitors but for some years Elizabeth prevaricated, inclining first to one and then to another. Ultimately, she chose to remain unmarried and died a spinster: 'the Virgin Queen'.

The disagreements between England and France continued, Catholic France remaining hostile to Protestant England. However, there was by now a great number of Protestants in France, called Huguenots (derived from a German word meaning 'confederates') who were trying to depose the French king and put a Protestant king on the throne. English relations with France were not helped by the fact that Elizabeth was ever ready to help the Huguenots and sent soldiers to fight for their cause. But there was another and more serious matter that further increased the enmity between England and France, the position of Mary, queen of Scots, to whose unhappy story we must now turn.

MARY QUEEN OF SCOTS

Mary Stuart had married Francis, the son of the king of France, and although she lived in France from an early age she was by right still the queen of Scotland. In 1559 Francis succeeded his father as king of France but within eighteen months he was dead. Mary, anxious to leave the French court, accepted an invitation of the Scottish Parliament to return to Scotland where at this time a fierce battle was taking place between the powerful Catholic party and the Protestants, led by the Puritan, John Knox.

On her return Mary chose a young nobleman called Henry Darnley as her second husband, but the marriage was not a success. Darnley was a dangerous rogue who, in a fit of jealousy, stabbed to death one of Mary's friends and as a result Mary came to hate her husband and was determined to be rid of him. Mary now wanted to marry the Earl of Bothwell and, when Darnley was killed by a gunpowder explosion in the queen's home where he was staying, no one doubted that his death had been brought about by Bothwell. Nevertheless, Mary immediately married him, providing the excuse for a major Protestant uprising against her which resulted in Bothwell fleeing to the Orkneys and Mary being captured and imprisoned. She escaped and raised an army, but was overwhelmingly defeated at Langside and went into hiding. Although she could have returned to France, somewhat surprisingly she decided to take refuge in England and trust to the goodwill of Elizabeth. From that day until her death nineteen years later she was kept a virtual prisoner because throughout that time she was considered a serious danger both to Elizabeth and to the Protestant cause.

The years that followed witnessed a period of conspiracy and intrigue. Plot after plot to have Mary substituted for Elizabeth as queen was hatched and failed as Mary was moved from one place of custody to another, although whether she was a party to any of these plots is uncertain. At some stage Elizabeth finally made up her mind that Mary would have to die because while she lived there existed a major threat both to the crown and the Protestant church.

In 1586, the Babington Conspiracy to kill the queen, free Mary and set up the Roman Catholic religion again with the help of Spanish troops from the Netherlands, was discovered. Whether or not Mary knew of this plan, it provided the excuse for her to be tried and convicted. The judges appointed by Elizabeth would listen to no arguments on Mary's behalf and she was duly sentenced to death. For some time Elizabeth was loath to sign the warrant for execution but finally she did so. Mary was brave to the end. On 8 February 1587 she was led to the scaffold maintaining that, after nearly twenty years of imprisonment, death was welcome and that she was glad to die for her religion. Thus ended the unfortunate life of Mary queen of Scots at the age of forty-five.

WAR WITH SPAIN: THE SPANISH ARMADA

If Elizabeth had troubles at home, she also had troubles abroad. At the beginning of her reign France was an enemy of England, although relations with Spain had become more friendly due to Mary Tudor's marriage to Phillip of Spain. Both these situations were to change.

In France, on 24 August 1572, the St Bartholomew's Day Massacre started when 40,000 Huguenot leaders and their followers were murdered, King Charles IX himself taking part in the killings. Henry of Navarre, the leader of the Huguenots, escaped and some years later finally got his revenge when, in 1590, he won a great victory at the Battle of Ivry and advanced to Paris. There he was welcomed and the people were prepared to accept him as king on condition he declared himself a Catholic. He consented with the words: 'Paris is worth a Mass' and he was duly crowned King Henry IV of France. But, although he had changed his religion to gain a kingdom, he remained a good friend of the Huguenots and issued the Edict of Nantes which gave the French Protestants the right to follow their own religion unhindered. More importantly, he remained a good friend to Elizabeth and to Protestant England, which explains the change of relations for the better between the two countries.

On the other hand, relations between England and Spain took an unfortunate turn for the worse. The years of Elizabeth's reign saw the beginning of world discoveries by the great sailors of that time. The Portuguese and Spaniards were the first off the mark, the Portuguese going east and the Spaniards west, conquering Mexico and parts of mainland America, the Spanish Main. Their ships were returning with immense riches from the gold and silver mines of Peru and sailing back with slaves from Africa to work in the heat of the new colonies. It did not take long for English sailors such as Frobisher, Drake and many others to decide that these colonies were not to be left to Spain alone, and a cruel and bloody struggle commenced. The Spaniards found themselves confronted by a nation of seamen who fought them fiercely for their booty and their possessions on the Main.

It was not to be supposed that Philip of Spain would tolerate these attacks for long. He was no fan of Elizabeth, having been one of her suitors in marriage whom had been refused, and he looked upon her and her people as heretics whom it was his duty to bring back to the old religion. And now the English sailors were burning Spanish ships, sacking Spanish colonies, seizing Spanish riches and, in the words of Francis Drake, 'doing all they could to singe the king of Spain's beard'. It was therefore not surprising that Philip resolved to strike one great blow against England which would protect Spain's seamen and possessions overseas and destroy the power of the English Protestant party once and for all.

Philip's plan was to collect a large army in the Netherlands and bring it across to England under the protection of a great fleet from Spain. England had no standing army and though its naval ships carried large cannons, they were relatively few in number. But when England stood in peril of invasion by a foreign enemy, religious differences were mostly forgotten and the country united to protect its shores. Volunteers came forward in their thousands, merchants provided further armed ships and fortifications were raised.

On 19 July 1558 the Spanish Armada of 131 ships set sail under the command of the Duke of Medina Sidonia. His orders were strict: he was to sail directly to Dunkirk to take on board the waiting army and then sail into the Thames estuary and land the troops. He was to stop for no man until he reached Dunkirk.

When the news came that the Armada was coming up the Channel, the captains of the warships were playing bowls on Plymouth Hoe: Drake, Hawkins, Frobisher, Grenville, Howard and Walter Raleigh among them. When they heard the news, instead of dashing off to their ships in the Sound, they famously agreed that 'there was time to finish the game first – and beat the Spaniards afterwards'.

The enemy was allowed to pass and was followed up the Channel before the fighting began. It soon became apparent that the big Spanish ships were no match in sailing or gunnery for the English, whose smaller ships were too fast for them and whose cannons were heavier and more powerful when harnessed to the new tactic of broadsides. The Spaniards eventually arrived at Dunkirk with a diminished fleet but when they lay at anchor that night two fireships, laden with explosives and inflammable material, were sailed in amongst them by two brave young captains, and were left to sail by themselves in a strong wind, creating havoc among the Spanish lines.

When the depleted Spanish fleet eventually sailed out of Dunkirk, a fierce battle raged and the Spaniards were heavily defeated. What was left of the great Armada was scattered by a gale into the North Sea where they attempted to return to Spain round Scotland, down the west coast of Ireland and into the Atlantic. But the rocky coasts and Atlantic rollers took a further toll. It was one of the most decisive victories in England's maritime history.

By the time of the defeat of the Spanish Armada, Elizabeth had reigned for thirty years. Although she remained unmarried she had always had her 'favourites' at court, including the Earl of Leicester, Sir Walter Raleigh, and Robert Devereux, second Earl of Essex. In 1599 Essex was sent to subdue the Irish who had been rebellious throughout her reign and where English dominance was now threatened by the Earl of Tyrone, Hugh O'Neil. Despite commanding the largest army ever sent to Ireland, Essex failed ignominiously, fell from grace and was finally executed at the behest of his enemies. These included Robert Cecil, son of the now deceased Lord Burleigh, who had succeeded his father as the queen's chief counsellor.

Elizabeth's reign was now drawing to a close. Old age was taking its toll and she had lost most of her indomitable spirit, falling into unhappy solitude. On 24 March 1603 Queen died at Richmond in her seventieth year. She was the last of the Tudors and left behind a country which under her authority had re-emerged as a major power in Europe, had returned from economic chaos to comparative prosperity and had become largely united under a common religious faith.

THE GLORIOUS YEARS

These were not the only inheritances bequeathed by the Tudor monarchs. The century or so between the death of Richard III on Bosworth Field and the death of Queen Elizabeth was a glorious one, witnessing the successful deeds of more great persons than any other in England's history.

It would be true to say that 'the world for every Englishman was doubled in size'. Throughout the sixteenth century bold seamen made adventurous journeys across unknown and perilous seas. Spain and Portugal led the way, the Dutch followed and later England took the lead. America, Canada, Mexico and Peru to the west, Africa to the south and India, Japan and even Australia to the east, were countries which were now included on maps of the world. Generally speaking it was after these great discoveries had been made by Christopher Columbus, Vasco da Gama, Cortez, Magellan and others that the English adventurers turned their attentions to these new lands. In the three years between 1577 and 1580, Drake sailed round the world in the *Golden Hind*, Sir Walter Raleigh started an English colony in Virginia, USA, and the queen claimed sovereignty over the New Found Land, the oldest colony in the British Empire. A company was formed to trade in the east, the East India Company, which became the all-powerful master of India.

The treasures and more earthly prizes that were retained from these distant places introduced for the first time to Europe luxuries which are considered commonplace today. Tobacco and the potato were brought by Raleigh from America in 1592, orange trees arrived from China, asparagus from Asia and cauliflower from Cyprus. Tea and coffee were to start arriving shortly afterwards. Englishmen for the first time were allowed to read the Bible and the Book of Common Prayer in their own language. Shakespeare was born in 1564 and between 1588 and 1610 wrote all his famous plays. Edmund Spenser wrote *The Fairie Queene*, the famous poem in six books of twelve chapters each, Francis Bacon wrote his celebrated *Essays*, and Thomas More *Utopia*. The period was also rich with other written works by such as Marlowe, Ben Jonson the Poet Laureate, Daniel and Massinger. The painting of portraits and other pictures began to be practised with increasing skill. Some of the most famous painters there have ever been lived during the Tudor period: Hans Holbein, Raphael, Titian and Michelangelo, to mention just a few.

Architects were designing and building the great private houses such as Longleat, Burghley and Montacute in what became known as the Tudor or Elizabethan style. Cardinal Wolsey founded Christ Church, Oxford, and many of England's famous schools date from this time including Harrow, Rugby, St Paul's and Westminster. The first public theatres appeared in London and the reconstructed Globe Theatre can still be seen in Southwark.

Hubert L Smith, Sir Walter Raleigh, reproduced by kind permission of the Provost and Fellows of Oriel College, Oxford.

Finally, Elizabeth's reign witnessed the changes made to the calendar by Pope Gregory XIII in 1582, though they were not at that time adopted by England. Before the time of Pope Gregory the new year started on 25 March and the celebrations traditionally commenced on that date with the giving of presents and ended with parties on 1 April. It was also known that the year was made up of 365 days plus a further short period of time reckoned to be six hours, but which in fact should have been eleven minutes and eleven seconds shorter. This had resulted in the calendar becoming out of order by nearly ten days and Gregory sought to put this right by commanding every country to begin to date everything ten days later and for the new year to commence on 1 January. England and some other countries unfriendly to the pope refused on principle to adopt the 'new style', which led to some confusion for the next 170 years because it was not until 1751 that the change was made in England. The change of date for the start of the year is also thought to be responsible for the origin of April Fool's Day, in that anyone who refused to accept or forgot the change was made fun of by being sent foolish presents and invitations to non-existent parties.

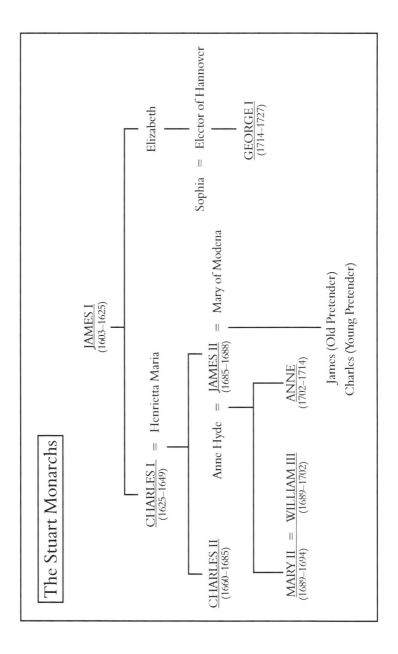

The Stuart Monarchs

JAMES I (1603–1625)

CHARLES I (1625–1649) = Henrietta Maria

Elizabeth = Elector of Hannover

Sophia = Elector of Hannover

GEORGE I (1714–1727)

CHARLES II (1660–1685)

Anne Hyde = JAMES II (1685–1688) = Mary of Modena

James (Old Pretender)

Charles (Young Pretender)

MARY II (1689–1694) = WILLIAM III (1689–1702)

ANNE (1702–1714)

V

The Stuarts (1603–1714)

i James I (1603–1625)

We now come to the Stuart period, which lasted 111 years (1603–1714).

Edward VI, Mary Tudor and Elizabeth had left no children, and James VI, King of Scotland and son of Mary Queen of Scots, became the rightful heir to the English throne.

Since the fourteenth century the sovereigns of Scotland had been members of the Stuart family and thus, when he succeeded to the throne of England as James I, the Stuart period commenced and he was to be followed by Charles I and Charles II, James II, Mary and Anne before it ended in 1714.

James was thirty-six years old when he arrived in great state as the first king of the four countries of the British Isles, happy to exchange the relatively austere palace of Holyrood for the greater splendour of Windsor and the Court of St James.

But he himself was an unattractive personality both in appearance and habits, ingratiating himself with a sycophantic court and considering himself king by divine right and as such above the law. As we shall see, this led to a fierce struggle between the king and Parliament which continued throughout the Stuart period and eventually resulted in the establishment of the power of Parliament as it is known today.

The Commons had always claimed the right to prevent the king from imposing taxes without their consent and on occasions had quite often refused to do so or had demanded something in return. But the Wars of the Roses had resulted in most of the great nobles being killed in battle or on the scaffold and, by the time the first of the Tudors ascended the throne at the end of the fifteenth century, Parliament was not strong enough to fight a powerful king without their support. So it was that during the reigns of the Tudors the power of the crown became greater than ever before and the Doctrine of Divine Right was created which declared that kings ruled as a matter of right and that this right was given to them by God.

But James was no Elizabeth, so he was mistaken when he thought he could step into her shoes and wield equivalent power, and it was not long before Parliament and the people declared that king had no divine right to rule over them and was not above the law. So began the struggle for democratic self-government over the old despotic order.

James' first Parliament started with a quarrel over the election of Sir Francis Goodwin as member for Buckinghamshire. The king disapproved of his election and prevailed upon the country to accept Sir John Fortescue instead. The Commons refused to allow Sir John to take his seat, but the king insisted, and the argument was finally compromised by holding a further election. The first skirmish in the great battle that was to take place during the Stuart period had ended in a draw. This first Parliament sat for nearly six years until 1610 when it was dissolved following its refusal to sanction higher import duties, thereby establishing the principle that the king could not raise taxes without Parliament's consent.

In the meantime there were other more pressing problems that required James' attention, spearheaded by the Elizabethan legacy of religious tolerance.

At that time there were three main religious parties in England: the Established Church, the Roman Catholics and the Puritans, who did not think the reforms of the Established Church went far enough and were therefore enemies of both the Protestants and the Catholics. When the new king arrived everyone was concerned to find out with which of these parties he would side with, and they did not have to wait for long. James soon made it clear that he intended to support the Established church and declared that, like Henry VIII, he was head of the church of England and that no one could lay down the teaching of that church better than himself. Having made up his mind, he was not slow to enforce the laws against all who opposed, Catholic and Puritans alike, and in consequence made enemies of both.

Although James was prepared to accept the existence of a large number of Catholics providing they caused no trouble, those who actively opposed his church, such as some of the more zealous priests and particularly the Jesuits, were vigorously dealt with. The position might have remained no worse than that had it not been for a group of zealots who confirmed James' worst fears by hatching the Gunpowder Plot.

The conspirators, led by Robert Catesby and including Guy Fawkes and others, devised a plan to blow up the king and the whole of Parliament by filling a cellar under the House of Lords with kegs of gunpowder. They hoped that this would lead to a Catholic rising with Spanish help and to the return of Catholicism in England. The plot nearly succeeded, but one of the conspirators had a friend in the House of Lords whom he warned by anonymous letter to be absent from the House on 5 November, the day that Parliament was meeting. This was enough to arouse suspicion, the premises were searched, and Guy Fawkes was arrested in the cellar with the taper in his hand ready to explode the gunpowder. Although tortured, he steadfastly refused to name his accomplices and he was executed on 1 February, 1606. But this did not save his companions, who were eventually arrested and suffered the same fate. Needless to say, the people of England were shocked and turned their anger upon the Catholics, many of whom were as indignant with the conspirators as any Protestant, and as a result the laws against the Catholics were made stricter and carried out more harshly. Parliament banned them from living anywhere near London and from holding public office, allowed the king to appropriate large parts of their lands, and demanded they swore an oath of allegiance to the crown. Those who refused were punished and persecuted with as much zeal as the Protestants had been in former days by the Roman Catholics.

During the first half of his reign James had the advantage of having Robert Cecil as his chief minister, but when he died in 1612 the king's ministers thereafter proved less worthy, being more concerned with their own interests than the welfare of the country. The two best-known were Robert Carr and George Villiers. Even Francis Bacon, one of the most intelligent of persons who became Lord Chancellor, was impeached for accepting bribes and sentenced to life imprisonment.

James had married Anne, daughter of the king of Denmark, and they had three children: Henry, who died aged nineteen, Charles, who was to become King Charles I, and Elizabeth, who was married in 1613 to Frederick V, the Elector Palatine, one of the Protestant princes of Germany who was elected king of Bohemia in 1618. By this time the Thirty Years' War between the Protestants and Catholics on the continent had broken out and Frederick was driven out of his new kingdom by his enemies and never recovered it, fighting the whole of his life for a crown he never possessed except in name. He was known as the 'Snow King' because his claims to royalty kept melting away. Frederick is mentioned particularly because his and Elizabeth's daughter Sophia married Ernest, Elector of Hanover, from whom the present royal family is directly descended.

There are a number of other events for which James' reign is particularly remembered.

First, the union between the crowns of England and Scotland. This was the first step towards the real union which exists today but which is in danger once more from the devolution policies of the current New Labour government. It must not be supposed that the union of the two crowns under James ended centuries of jealousy and enmity. Battles between the English and Scottish armies were still to be fought, old prejudices remained and each still regarded the other as foreigners. But the first step towards real union had taken place and good will and good sense were ultimately to prevail.

Second, the settling in the north of Ireland of a number of Englishmen and Scots sent over by James to occupy the lands which had become vacant in Ulster through fighting and insurrection. James' intention was to strengthen the Protestant cause by 'colonising' the province of Ulster with a loyal Protestant population. This he did successfully and thereby sowed the seeds for the religious violence that has plagued Ireland in recent years.

Third, the Bible was translated into English and became the only version to be allowed by law to be used in the churches. Today the Revised Version is read, which is the same except for some small errors of translation which have been corrected and which still contains the Preface in which the translators dedicate their work to 'the most high and mighty Prince James'.

Fourth, the death of Sir Walter Raleigh in 1618. At the beginning of James' reign Sir Walter had been convicted of plotting with Lord Cobham to get help from Spain and was imprisoned in the Tower. His quarters in the White Tower can be visited today and still contain the desk at which he wrote *A Historie of the World*. In 1617 he was finally released and sent off to head an expedition to Guiana to find the fabled city of El Dorado. He failed to find the golden city and came to blows with the Spaniards who were already established there. At the time England was at peace with Spain and on his return his enemies accused him of making war. Although this offence was not punishable by death, his original sentence of fourteen years before was revived and under that sentence he was condemned to death and executed in 1618.

Finally, Shakespeare died in 1616; the Puritan Pilgrim Fathers set sail from Plymouth in 1620 in the *Mayflower* and settled in New England; Inigo Jones designed the first of his great classical buildings; and Rubens and Van Dyck established themselves among the greatest of the European painters.

ii   Charles 1 (1625–1649)

When Charles I came to the throne he was twenty-five years old, handsome, shy and artistic. He immediately married Henrietta Maria, daughter of the king of France, after whom Maryland in America was named. Like his father, he strongly believed in his divine right to rule and almost immediately set out on a collision course with Parliament which was eventually to result in civil war and the decade of the Republic under Cromwell. It was a time when two contrasting sets of people grew up side by side: Cavaliers with their fine clothes and extravagant behaviour and the Roundheads (or Puritans) with their cropped hair, sombre dress and strict rules of life. Each group despised the other.

It was also a time when the Protestants and Catholics in Europe were engaged in the fierce Thirty Years' War and, although Charles was a Protestant and Head of the Established Church, his French wife was a Catholic and he was anxious maintain friendly relations with his father-in-law, the king of France. He therefore had Catholic sympathies and, with the support of his chief minister, Buckingham, favoured the High Church party of William Laud who was made Archbishop of Canterbury shortly afterwards.

On the other hand, Parliament was becoming increasingly Puritan and when Charles' first Parliament was called, it registered displeasure both at his marriage and at Buckingham. But far worse for Charles, it refused to vote him the king's customary income from import duties ('tunnage and poundage') for life, voting it for one year only. Charles was furious and rather than take it on such conditions, he refused it altogether.

Relations with Parliament were further strained when he tried to help King Louis in his war with the French Protestants, the Huguenots. A fleet of ships had been collected to help the Huguenots besieged in La Rochelle, but the ships were ordered by Charles to take aboard French soldiers and to help the Catholic besiegers rather than the Protestant besieged.

It was not long before another conflict arose over money. Without his 'tunnage and poundage', Charles was in desperate need of income and again Parliament was asked to vote subsidies. Not only was Parliament angry with the king for trying to help the French Catholics, but they were also angry with Buckingham who was felt to be responsible, and again they refused to vote a penny unless a list of their grievances, one of which was to get rid of Buckingham, was addressed. Charles' reaction to this was to dissolve this first Parliament and to start on the road to despotism that was to lead to his downfall and ultimately his death.

Sir Anthony Van Dyck, King Charles I in Three Positions, The Royal Collection, © 2006, Her Majesty Queen Elizabeth II. Photograph by SC.

To get the money he needed, Charles raised a 'forced loan' without the approval of Parliament and imprisoned those who refused to pay, in flagrant breach of the law. It was therefore hardly surprising that he was then compelled to summon his second Parliament in 1626, which met in an even more determined frame of mind. Additions were made to the original list of grievances, headed by the continued insistence that Buckingham must be removed. The king then took a very foolish step by refusing to allow Parliament to question Buckingham and threatened that unless they 'hastened his supplies [money], it would be the worse for them'. Parliament replied by declaring it was their right and duty to enquire into the conduct of the king's ministers and it thus became one of the chief principles of England's Constitution that ministers of the Crown should be answerable to Parliament. When Parliament went further and impeached Buckingham, Charles promptly dissolved it once again.

Although Charles got rid of a troublesome House of Commons he still had not got his money and once more he resorted to illegal means by extorting money without the consent of Parliament, by orders under the Great Seal. In this he had the support of Bishop Laud and, to widespread dismay, the then Chief Justice Sir Nicholas Hyde ruled that the law had not been broken when Charles imprisoned five gentlemen for refusing to pay.

In March 1628 Charles was compelled to call together his third Parliament. Once again the king asked for money and once again Parliament replied that 'grievances and supplies should go hand in hand'.

This time their main grievances were drawn up in a petition to the king, known as the Petition of Right, which included the provisions that no man should be compelled to pay taxes to the king without the consent of Parliament and that no man should be imprisoned without 'cause shown'. The king at first prevaricated, but in his desperation for the much-needed cash he finally gave way and signed the petition. However, when it came to putting the king's promises to the test he was found to be as obstinate as ever. He now declared that tunnage and poundage were not taxes and that he would levy them whether the Commons liked it or not. The House of Commons of course objected and this time found itself 'prorogued' (adjourned) rather than dissolved. The Commons refused to adjourn and on 2 March 1629 a second royal message was sent with the same command. The Speaker, Sir John Finch, was a friend of the king's, but the doors were locked, the Speaker forcibly held down in his chair to prevent him reading the king's command and resolutions passed declaring the House's determination to uphold the liberties claimed in the Petition of Right. Charles immediately dissolved Parliament and punished those who had been chiefly responsible. Eleven years were to pass before Parliament was summoned again.

The king then once more attempted to rule as an absolute monarch with the help of Lord Wentworth, later made Earl of Strafford, and Laud, who was appointed Archbishop of Canterbury in 1633. It was therefore not surprising that his troubles still continued.

Lack of money meant that England had been forced to retire from the power struggles of Europe and had lost its authority abroad. In trying to remedy this, the king only succeeded in further increasing his unpopularity by the raising of 'ship money' to provide a number of vessels to help the king of Spain against the Dutch.

The Court of Star Chamber was revived by Laud to deal with those who broke the strict laws of the Established Church, and many were tried and severely punished, particularly the Puritans whose party was growing in strength day by day.

But it was not until Laud was rash enough to try to compel the Scots to accept the rules and services of the Church of England that he actually drove his enemies into civil war. The Scottish Presbyterians were affronted and drew up a declaration called the 'Solemn League and Covenant' which was signed by thousands who became known as the Covenanters and who raised an army and marched to the border. Charles, with no money to raise troops, could do nothing except make a truce and agree to pay their costs as soon as Parliament met and in this way was forced, much against his will, to call his fourth Parliament. This Parliament sat for only twenty-three days and still refused to vote any money unless their grievances were settled. But when the Scots marched into

Northumberland and Durham, the king had no choice but to summon his fifth and last Parliament, the Long Parliament that was destined to sit for no less than nineteen years.

The Long Parliament met on 3 November 1640, starting its life powerless and despised. Its first act was to attack the hated Strafford by a Bill of Attainder, a bill passed by both Houses in which the person accused was declared guilty of high treason and sentenced to death. Capital punishment required the consent of the king and in this case, to his everlasting shame, Charles gave the consent which resulted in his most faithful servant being executed on 12 May 1641.

The House of Commons then impeached Laud who was tried and imprisoned, but not executed until four years later. Others who had assisted the king in his illegal actions were also punished, 'ship money' was declared illegal, the Court of Star Chamber was abolished and a bill was passed providing that a Parliament should be held at least every three years.

The struggle between king and Parliament had now reached such a stage that civil war had become inevitable. On 4 January 1642 six members of Parliament were charged by the king with treason and the king himself with a troop of soldiers entered the House of Commons to arrest them. But they had been warned to keep away and the king, mortified and angry, left to shouts of 'Privilege! Privilege!' which meant he had acted contrary to the rules and privileges of the House. Finally, against the king's wishes but for their own protection, Parliament claimed the right to command the army and navy and without the king's consent passed the Militia Bill. On 23 April 1642 the first act of civil war took place. On that day the commander at Hull refused to obey the king's order to hand over arms and ammunition stored in the town and shut the gates against the king.

On 22 August 1642 Charles raised his standard at Nottingham. The head of the Parliamentary army was the

Earl of Essex, son of Elizabeth's suitor, and under him was an officer called Oliver Cromwell who was to play so great a part in the war and events that followed. The king's party, the Cavaliers, were experienced in fighting, while the Parliamentary party, the Roundheads, were unaccustomed to battle. It was therefore not surprising that to start with the Parliamentary troops suffered many defeats, the first being at the battle of Edgehill in Oxfordshire. Two principal factors caused the tide to ultimately turn. First, the Roundheads arranged for armed assistance from the Scottish Covenanters and second, Oliver Cromwell had trained a body of some 20,000 well-disciplined soldiers, known as the New Model Army, under the command of Sir Thomas Fairfax. Cromwell himself commanded the regiment of cavalry, Cromwell's Ironsides, who were never beaten and are still considered as the most formidable cavalry the world has ever seen.

The New Model Army was first in action at the battle of Naseby in Northamptonshire in June 1645 when the king's army was resoundingly defeated, and within twelve months the war was effectively over. The king sought protection with the Scottish army which by now had marched as far south as Nottingham, but for a payment of £400,000 he was handed over to the Parliamentary army in January 1647 and thereafter held prisoner at various locations.

Up to this time there had been only two parties, one for the king and the other for Parliament, who were mostly Presbyterians. But during the civil war a new party had begun to rise, the Independence Party, which was really the party of the army. The Independents went further than the Presbyterians in their hatred of the bishops and the king, and many of them held very strict Puritan views and were republicans who wished to see the country governed without a king.

After the capture of the king the differences between the Independents and the Presbyterians increased more than ever. Parliament attempted to disband the army without pay, and in August 1647 the army marched to London to become masters of the situation. Fairfax then defeated the king's friends in Kent and Cromwell destroyed the Scottish army at Preston.

The army then turned its attentions to Parliament and on 6 December 1648 Colonel Pride, with a troop of cavalry, marched to the House of Commons and arrested or debarred all but about sixty Independents. For the next five years the remaining members, the Rump, were the only representatives of the people in the Commons and they were prepared to do exactly what they were required to do by the army.

Their first act was to pass a bill declaring it high treason to make war upon Parliament and on 20 January 1649 the king was brought before his judges in Westminster Hall. The trial lasted several days and Charles bore himself with courage and dignity, but from the beginning the court had made up its mind and in due course the inevitable sentence of death was passed. It was carried out on 30 January outside the banqueting hall in Whitehall, the executioner holding up the severed head and crying: 'Here is the head of a traitor'. But it might be truly said that 'nothing in the king's life became him like the leaving of it', and, although his enemies looked upon him as a traitor, now that he was gone the people began to look on him more as a martyr and henceforth the Royalist party, though defeated and powerless for a time, gradually became stronger until once more it was the strongest party in the land.

iii The Commonwealth (1649–1660)

On the death of Charles the Independence Party, with Oliver Cromwell at its head, was all-powerful in the land. There was no force that could stand against the victorious army and support the young Charles, Prince of Wales, who was nineteen years old. Indeed, Parliament declared that to speak of him as king was treason and an act was passed declaring England henceforth to be a republic, a council of forty-one members being appointed to carry on government with John Milton, the poet, as its secretary.

Anarchy threatened. A feeling of revulsion at the execution of the king and the rule by force of the Independent ministry led to widespread unease. In addition, Ireland rebelled and in Scotland the Prince of Wales was proclaimed king of Great Britain. But Cromwell was prompt in acting to maintain his authority, personally leading an army to ruthlessly crush the Irish, and the following year, in September 1650, he routed the Scottish army at Dunbar. While Cromwell was fighting the Scots, Charles took the opportunity to hurry south and march towards London. But Cromwell reacted in time, caught up with the royal army at Worcester and decisively defeated Charles. However, he managed to escape and avoided capture for six weeks before finally reaching the coast of France in safety. At one time he famously avoided capture by hiding in the branches of an oak tree while his pursuers galloped past underneath, resulting thereafter in a great deal of public houses being called the Royal Oak.

Ireland had now been subjugated, Scotland was quiet under the strong rule of George Monck and in England all Royalist resistance had been put to an end by their defeat at Worcester. The real power was in Cromwell's hands rather than Parliament's, which now consisted only of the depleted House of Commons, the House of Lords having been abolished in the first year of the Commonwealth. This Parliament had already sat for thirteen years and had little power and few friends, but without a king or upper House there was no power to dissolve it legally and it was therefore decided that it should be dissolved by force.

On 20 April 1653 Cromwell, still a member of Parliament himself, entered the Chamber with thirty soldiers, removed the mace which was the House's symbol of authority and ejected the Speaker and the members. The Rump of the Long Parliament was thus ended by the army it had helped to create and Cromwell became the ruler of England in name as well as in fact. In December 1653 a proclamation was issued declaring Cromwell to be 'Lord Protector of the Commonwealth' helped by a Council of fifteen members. Following a series of attempted Royalist plots, in 1655 twelve of the army's major generals were appointed to govern twelve districts into which England was divided, and for the time being there was peace.

The next year Cromwell successfully assisted the Protestants in Italy and the British fleet took the island of Jamaica, defeating the Spanish fleet and capturing a great convoy of treasure that it was escorting. This popular success abroad led Cromwell to decide to do away with government by the major generals and once more to summon a Parliament and to re-institute the House of Lords. But within a year, when the House of Commons ventured to oppose him, he once again dissolved it and thereafter reigned as an absolute dictator until his death on 3 September 1658.

Whatever may be thought of him, there is no doubt that he made England more powerful and respected than it had been for many years. He had shown himself to be a strong ruler both at home and abroad and was never more powerful and more respected than just before his death.

The Commonwealth dream died with Cromwell, whose son Richard ('Tumbledown Dick') took over as Lord Protector, but within months Charles II was heading for the throne. The people of England had got rid of the king not because they hated kings, but because they hated a king who oppressed them and broke the law. Now that they found that government without a king meant military rule with oppression and law breaking thrown into the bargain, they were ready to go back to try once more government by king, Lords and Commons.

The way back was led by General Monck. He, it will be remembered, had been left in Scotland to keep that country in order. He marched with his small army across the border to London where he declared he was in favour of a 'free Parliament', was acclaimed by the city, and the Long Parliament was ended for ever. So it came about that a free Parliament was once again elected, the views of moderate men being heard for the first time for many years, and it was time for the return of the king. On 26 May 1660 Charles landed at Dover with every sign of acclaim from the people of England because it was felt that a great weight had been lifted from the country and that it was a welcome day which saw the end of government by a despotic ruler and the restoration of the monarchy.

iv   Charles II (1660–1685)

Although the country was ready to welcome the young king and to forget the faults of his father, scarcely had the bells ceased ringing when it was seen that many difficulties had to be overcome before the mantle of peace could lie easily over the country. Charles was easy-going and charming, clever but unwise and determined to pursue the agreeable lifestyle of a libertine. Nell Gwyn was one of his many mistresses and he was said to have sired at least fourteen bastards, causing Pepys to observe: 'he cannot command himself in the presence of any woman he likes'. It was therefore hardly surprising that he was content to leave the government of the country to his chief minister, Edward Hyde, Earl of Clarendon. Although efforts were made to prevent the Royalists taking revenge on their enemies it was impossible to prevent them from punishing those who had been directly responsible for the death of Charles I. Many were put to death and even the body of Cromwell was taken from his grave and hanged at Tyburn.

Charles had a French mother and a brother, James, Duke of York, both of whom were Catholics. It was therefore hardly surprising that he sympathised with the Catholics and wanted to protect them although the Established Church had once again been set up.

Parliament was summoned in the first year of Charles' reign and was largely composed of Cavaliers who immediately passed several bills to suppress the Puritans. However, tunnage and poundage was regranted to the king for life and for the first time the monarch was allowed to keep a force of regular soldiers in time of peace. The two regiments that composed this standing army became known as the 'Royal Scots' and the 'Coldstream Guards'.

In 1662 the Act of Uniformity was passed which compelled every clergyman to accept the form of service used in the prayer book. Those who refused were turned out of their livings, lost their civil rights and many were imprisoned or deported.

But it was Charles' policy abroad that was his principal disaster. He picked a quarrel with Holland and declared war in 1665 at a time when the English fleet was ill-equipped and ill-prepared. As a result they were heavily defeated in a battle which took place in the Channel and within eighteen months the Dutch fleet sailed into the mouth of the Medway virtually unopposed and administered the final humiliation by burning what was left of the Navy.

Meanwhile in 1665 a terrible plague broke out in London, spread rapidly through the narrow dirty streets, and caused the death of over 100,000 people. This was followed the next year by the Great Fire of London which broke out in Pudding Lane on 2 September 1666 and raged for nearly five days, burning more than 13,000 houses and eighty-nine churches to the ground. Although this was a major disaster at least it provided an opportunity to rebuild a splendid city to replace the maze of unplanned crooked streets. Alas, this opportunity was not taken. Although the great architect Christopher Wren planned a new city of London, his plans were refused and Wren was left to build his many churches including St Paul's Cathedral.

It was widely believed that the plague and the fire had been sent as judgements to punish the country for the wickedness of the court, and it was therefore not surprising that it was Clarendon who first felt the anger of the people and only succeeded in saving his life by fleeing the country. For the next six years Charles governed through a council nicknamed 'The Cabal' after the initial letters of the names of the five members: Clifford, Arlington, Buckingham, Ashley (afterwards Lord Shaftesbury) and Lauderdale. It later became formally known as the 'Cabinet', a name it has held ever since. Three of the members were supporters of religious tolerance and two were Catholics, which gave rise to some alarm as the great majority of the people were Protestants who feared Catholic France and wished to be friends with Protestant Holland. When the king and his Cabinet entered into an alliance with France and another Dutch war began, Charles' popularity began to wane. His position was made worse when, in 1673, he issued a 'Declaration of Indulgence' pardoning those who had offended against the Act of Uniformity and granting toleration of all, including the Catholics. This was too much for Parliament, who compelled Charles to withdraw the Declaration and passed the Test Act under which no one could hold any office of state who did not declare himself a member of the Established Church. This meant that the two Catholic members of the Cabinet, Clifford and Arlington, had to resign and, as a result, the 'Cabal' government came to an end and for the first time in England's history the king had to accept a chief minister from the party which held the majority in Parliament. This was the Earl of Danby, a strong Anglican, who immediately made peace with Holland and arranged for the Duke of York's daughter, Mary, who was a Protestant, to marry William of Orange, leader of the Dutch Protestants and bitter enemy of Louis XIV of France.

Nevertheless, the Protestants in England still feared the Catholics and believed them to be a serious threat to the throne. This belief was strengthened in 1678 by the discovery of the Popish Plot that was revealed by Titus Oates, who swore that the object of the plot was to murder the king, destroy the Protestant Church and place the Catholic Duke of York on the throne. This conspiracy may well have been invented by Titus Oates because it was never definitively proved, although in the panic that ensued many innocent Catholics were sent to their deaths or imprisoned on his testimony. The Duke of York himself was compelled to give up his office as Lord High Admiral, and the Duke of Monmouth, the bastard son of Charles, was put forward as heir to the throne simply because he was Protestant.

In 1679 a new Parliament under the leadership of Shaftesbury passed the Habeas Corpus Act, which prevented illegal imprisonment and ensured that no man was kept in prison who had not been fairly tried and convicted. Any person in prison could demand as of right from the court a 'writ of habeas corpus', which directed the gaoler to 'take his body' before the court and to justify his custody. It remains to this day one of the greatest safeguards of our liberties.

The same Parliament passed an Exclusion Act which excluded James' succession to the throne, but the Lords rejected it and Charles dissolved Parliament for the last time. He was to govern without one for the last five years of his reign.

All these quarrels and disputes divided the country more and more and in 1683 the Rye House Plot, this time a Protestant plan to murder the king and set up a Republic, resulted in the beheading of leading Protestants and the return of the Duke of York to office.

King Charles died on 6 February 1685, adding further proof to the deceit of his reign by declaring on his deathbed that he was a Roman Catholic. Although his years on the throne were troubled times and yet again religious feelings created unrest and unhappiness, they should also be remembered for Bunyan's *Pilgrim's Progress*, Milton's *Paradise Lost* and the paintings of Rembrandt. A young Samuel Pepys was writing his Diaries, Isaac Newton was Professor of Mathematics at Cambridge and the Royal Society was incorporated.

It is said that James, Duke of York, once asked his brother, the king, if he was not afraid of being assassinated. 'No, no, Jamie,' said Charles, 'they'll never kill me to make you king.' He was right. Charles as king was not loved, but the people of England were soon to hate his brother.

v   James II (1685–1688)

James was a foolish rather than a bad man and perhaps he suffered more for his mistakes than his crimes. He was neither a great nor a wise man, but he was ready to take risks to promote his ideas of what was right. Unfortunately, when he tried to govern England in a manner which he thought was right, but which the people of England had long ago decided was altogether wrong, he faced an impossible task.

He was a Roman Catholic, friend of the French king and believed steadfastly in the 'Doctrine of Divine Right'. His people, on the other hand, were predominantly Protestants, hated the French, and had long ago determined that their king should only rule according to law and the will of Parliament. The ingredients for a disastrous reign were in place and it was not long before the storm clouds began to gather.

James, it must be remembered, was also king of Scotland and one of his first moves was to insist that the laws against the Scottish Covenanters should be strictly enforced. In the end, many thousands of Covenanters who dared to practise their religious beliefs openly were persecuted with extreme cruelty and in many cases put to death. This led to an insurrection breaking out, led by the Duke of Argyle, which was put down by the king's forces. Argyle was taken prisoner and executed. At the same time, during the first year of James' reign, a further uprising took place in England when the Duke of Monmouth, the bastard son of Charles II, landed at Lyme Regis in Dorset with eighty followers in an attempt to seize the throne. He hoped and believed that English Protestants would rally to his cause, but up to this time King James had done little to offend them and they were in no mood for the throne to be seized by force. Monmouth was therefore joined by only a few thousand untrained peasants and yeomen.

Lord Churchill, afterwards to become famous as the Duke of Marlborough and one of England's greatest generals, raised a force on behalf of the king and hurried west. At Sedgemore in Somerset the rebels were comprehensively defeated and Monmouth was captured and taken to London. Although he begged James for mercy, none was shown and he was beheaded shortly afterwards. The king then sent Judge Jeffreys, known for his severe and cruel sentences, to Exeter to try those survivors who had joined the rebellion. The trials were conducted without justice or mercy; hundreds were hanged, tortured or sold as slaves and it is still remembered as the 'Bloody Assizes'.

James now felt more secure on his throne and felt the

time had come when he could bring about the abolition of the Test Act, which had been passed in the reign of Charles II in order to deny public office to all those who refused to declare themselves members of the Established Church. But Parliament, predominantly Protestant, refused to pass the bill brought in to repeal the Test Act. James was furious and, following his principle of 'Divine Right', declared he had the power to dispense with any particular law and in this belief he was supported by the judges. James at once appointed Roman Catholics to a number of influential posts, including the Earl of Tryconnel, a violent and cruel soldier, who was made one of the king's chief ministers.

In 1687 the earl was sent to Ireland as Lord Lieutenant where he openly took up the cause of the Roman Catholics and set about oppressing the Protestants, which soon plunged Ireland once more into civil war.

To further his unpopularity, on 4 April 1687 James issued a proclamation called the 'Declaration of Indulgence' which did away with all punishments against those who had broken the Test Act. This gave a pardon not only to Catholics but also to Nonconformists and therefore supported the correct principle that no man should be punished for his religious opinions. But once again James did the right thing in the wrong way, by acting without the consent of Parliament. He even gave orders that the Declaration should be publicly read in all churches and, when the bishops of the Established Church refused to do so, seven were arrested and sent to the Tower.

Discontent in the country was now rising steadily and riots broke out in London, causing James to post a contingent of soldiers at Hounslow in case of further trouble. But when the seven bishops were acquitted by the Court of King's Bench they were enthusiastically welcomed back by the people of London and even the king's soldiers at Hounslow cheered at the news.

However, no warning appeared sufficient to make the king understand that his position was in jeopardy and, heedless of the consequences, he then proceeded to remove the Protestant heads of Oxford and Cambridge universities and to replace them with Catholics. It was now clear that the king's throne was tottering and it was in fact to fall within the year.

James had two daughters, Mary and Anne, by his first wife Anne Hyde. Mary, the eldest, was a Protestant and married to William Prince of Orange, son of the king of Holland. But in June 1688 James' second wife gave birth to a son, James Edward, who became the true heir to the throne. Those who were preparing to desert the king and support the Protestant Mary saw the newly arrived Prince of Wales as a danger and were moved to act quickly. Senior ministers and persons of influence had already been negotiating with William and Mary and promising support and, on 10 October 1658, William of Orange announced that he was about to land in England to take the place of his father-in-law on the throne and proclaim a free and legal Parliament.

On 5 November William landed at Torbay. An army under the Earl of Marlborough was sent to stop him but Marlborough and many other officers deserted to the Protestant cause.

James was forced to flee from London and escape to France. William, arriving in the capital unopposed, placed his cause in the hands of Parliament. The House of Commons then declared that King James, having broken the law and withdrawn from the country, had abdicated and that 'the throne had thereby become vacant'.

The claim of the child Prince of Wales was disallowed and the next heir, Mary, refused to become queen unless her husband also became king. Parliament acceded to this request and on 13 February 1689, William and Mary were proclaimed joint sovereigns, sharing royal responsibilities, and hence the expression for sharing became 'going Dutch'. Protestant Stuart had succeeded Catholic Stuart but there were still some stormy seas ahead.

vi William and Mary (1689–1702)

Although William and Mary were welcomed to the throne, particularly by the Protestants, it must not be supposed that England's troubles were over. There was no great affection for Mary, who had driven her own father from the throne, and William was a foreigner with unattractive manners who was obsessed with destroying the power of France.

England was a country divided by a number of different parties, the two principal ones being the Whigs and the Tories. The Whigs were a reforming party who believed in the supremacy of Parliament and therefore had played a major part in the deposing of James II. The name 'Whig' derives from the Scottish word *Whiggamore*, the nickname given to the rebels who marched to Edinburgh earlier in the seventeenth century. They were ready to support William, provided he chose his ministers from their party.

The Tories, on the other hand, mostly believed in the divine right and were strong supporters of the Established Church. Needless to say they also wanted the king's ministers to be appointed from their party. The word 'Tory' comes from the Irish word *Toraidhe* meaning outlaw, used to describe dispossessed Irish peasants forced to live as robbers, and was therefore an abusive nickname.

But however much the two parties differed they were both bitterly opposed to King James and therefore agreed that King William must be kept on the throne.

The first troubles started in Ireland where Tryconnel still held the country for King James and his Catholic supporters, called 'Jacobites', the king's name being Jacobus in Latin. Tryconnel now stepped up his oppression of the Protestants, a large number of whom took refuge in Londonderry, which came under siege. The king of France sent troops to assist Tryconnel and King James himself went over to lend his support directly. Londonderry held out bravely for 105 days and was ultimately saved when reinforcements from England sailed up the river, broke the boom and relieved the city.

A few months later William himself entered the fray and led an English and Dutch army over to Ireland. On 1 July 1690 he won a decisive victory over James at the Battle of the Boyne and James fled to France, never to return. Within a year William had established his authority in Ireland, but the bitter memories of this conflict between Protestants and Catholics still live on and provide the roots for the violent dissension that has continued unresolved to present times.

With Ireland subdued William was now free to continue his obsessive war against France. However, while he had been in Ireland the French had taken advantage of his absence and a large French fleet defeated the English off Beachy Head and took control of the Channel.

William now sent troops to Holland to help the Dutch against the French and several battles took place, with varying success. Marlborough was a very popular commander of the English forces, but he was an ambitious man and jealous of the Dutch generals to whom William was always showing favour. He quickly became angry and discontented and prepared for the second time to betray his king by writing letters of support to King James in France. But, far worse, he actually leaked information to the French of an intended English expedition against Brest and helped to bring about a major English defeat. When this was discovered, Marlborough was disgraced and forced to leave the court.

But an event now took place which finally ended the hopes of the Jacobites. In 1692 the French marshalled a large fleet for the invasion of England but James, with his usual lack of good judgement, issued a proclamation declaring that any Englishman who did not support him would be deemed a traitor. He also named hundreds from all parties whom he declared he would never pardon. Not surprisingly this had the effect of joining all parties together to resist the ex-king who was returning with a French army behind him and with threats of widespread punishment. The English and Dutch fleets united and on 1 May 1692 the French fleet was defeated.

The war in Holland nevertheless continued and the cost became greater all the time, so that William's determination to carry on his campaign against the French forced England into another financial crisis. Because of this, in 1692 a Whig called Charles Montague arranged a government loan of one million pounds which became known as the National Debt. Two years later Montague also set up a company with its 1268 shareholders subscribing £1.2 million which was then loaned to the government at 8% interest. But as it was illegal to lend the king money without the consent of Parliament, a Royal Charter was issued called 'The Governor and Company of the Bank of England', which is the origin of the Bank of England and why its head is called the Governor.

In 1694 Queen Mary died of smallpox aged thirty-two and William now reigned as sole monarch. The war continued for three more years. At last a truce was signed in September 1697 and in 1700 the Tories obtained a majority in Parliament and a new Tory government was formed.

Mary had died childless and the following year the Act of Settlement was passed which provided that, if the queen's sister Anne should die without heirs, the crown should go to the next Protestant heir and not to James II's son, or 'the Pretender' as he was called. There has been no Catholic monarch of England since that day.

In 1701 the war on the continent broke out again. William, always eager to strike against his old enemy Louis XIV, sent over 100,000 troops to Holland, headed by Marlborough, who had now been restored to favour. But just as it appeared that William's long-cherished hopes of crushing the French might be fulfilled, on 20 February 1702 he fell from his horse when it stumbled on a mole hill and died from his injuries shortly afterwards.

He was a man with few friends and many enemies, with many faults and some great virtues. He was a silent, determined and unpopular king but after his death all those who cared for good government, for religious tolerance and for the independence of England recognised that William of Orange had been a good, if not a great, king of England.

vii Anne (1702–1714)

Anne was the second daughter of James II and the sister of Queen Mary who left no children. By right the crown should have gone to James' son, but we have seen how Mary was placed on the throne by means of a 'revolution' and the Act of Succession was passed to ensure that the crown could only be worn by a Protestant. Everybody, therefore, except the Jacobites, now looked upon Anne as the rightful heir to the throne, although the Pretender remained a danger in the background with the support of the powerful French.

The two great parties, the Whigs and the Tories, had grown ever further apart. The Whigs were still determined to limit the power of the crown and to continue the war with France. The Tories, on the other hand, were ready to give more power to the monarch and were not in favour of the war. Although they were ready to support Anne they had no love for the next heirs to the throne, the Electress Sophia and her son George of Hanover.

Anne had always been a friend of the Duchess of Marlborough and now, with her husband the Duke, they became persons of great power and influence. Although Anne favoured the Tories and a Tory administration was formed under Lord Godolphin, Marlborough's son-in-law, Marlborough himself wanted to continue the war with France. This was not only because he was a brilliant general but also because he saw the dangers to England if Louis XIV should become master of all Europe.

The war therefore raged for almost the whole of Anne's reign. It was known as the 'War of the Spanish Succession' because King Louis wanted to make his grandson king of Spain and the enemies of France were determined to prevent this amalgamation of power in Europe. Marlborough's power was so great that for these reasons he was able to persuade the queen and the Tories to carry on the conflict.

It was a memorable war for England. The Duke of Marlborough, most brilliant of all English soldiers, headed an army of English, Dutch and Germans with Prince Eugene of Savoy a talented and loyal deputy. Marlborough had no intention of being tied down to another stalemate war in the Netherlands and in 1704 marched to the Danube, where he joined the Austrians and at Blenheim routed the French and Bavarian army. It was a catastrophic blow to Louis and led to the rapid decline of his power. All England, except the Tories, rejoiced and the queen rewarded Marlborough with Blenheim Palace, which she commissioned the architect Vanbrugh to build at her expense.

Other victories followed including Ramilles, Turin, Oudenarde, and Malplaquet. But the greatest prize won by England in this war was attained with the utmost ease. In 1704 an English fleet attacked Gibraltar, held by the Spanish allies of Louis XIV, and captured it almost without resistance. A rock fortress guarding the entrance to the

Mediterranean, it was of great strategic importance and has remained in British hands ever since.

Blenheim Palace, Oxfordshire, England; photograph by Tim Graham, Tim Graham Photo Library.

Nevertheless the power of the Marlboroughs was not to last. Despite his victories the Tories were opposed to the war with France and it was only Marlborough's influence with the queen through his wife that enabled him to carry it on. But the queen was becoming tired of the Duchess's sniping tongue and quarrelsome temper, and the Duke found his old Tory friends were slipping away, causing him to look to the Whigs for support. This was to no avail and when the Tories obtained a large majority in a new Parliament with Harley, Earl of Oxford, as prime minister, the fate of the Marlboroughs was finally sealed. The Duchess was dismissed from the court and the Duke deprived of his command with numerous charges being brought against him.

The last step was to end the war with France. On 31 March

1713 the Treaty of Utrecht was signed and the long struggle between England and France was ended for the time being. The terms of the peace were not altogether favourable to England but at least it gave the country three important possessions: Minorca, Gibraltar and Newfoundland.

While the war had been going on, a very important event had taken place about which the Whigs and Tories were, for once, in agreement. In 1707 the Act of Union between England and Scotland was passed. Although the crown of each country had been worn by the same king or queen since James I, there had been very little real union. Indeed, bitter disputes had regularly taken place. But now good sense prevailed and terms for a union were formally agreed and passed by the parliaments of both countries with large majorities, and the kingdom of Great Britain was established. Some of the other principal provisions of the act included that their parliaments should be united, sitting at Westminster with forty-five Scottish members in the Commons and sixteen peers in the Lords. The Act also decreed that the flags of the two countries (the red cross of St George and the white diagonal cross of St Andrew) should be joined together. But it was not until 1801, after the union with Ireland, that the red diagonal cross of St Patrick was added to result in the Union Jack as we know it today.

In 1713 the queen's health was failing and she had no child to succeed her. There was a real danger that the Pretender might return because he still had supporters, one of whom was believed to be Anne's chief minister, Lord Bolingbroke. The Whigs were so alarmed that they decided to take positive action to forestall this possible scenario and the Dukes of Argyle and Somerset, exercising their right as privy councillors, sought audience with the queen as she lay dying. They persuaded her that the Protestant cause which she had always supported would be lost if the Act of Settlement was not followed and the Elector of Hanover was not made king on her death. The only way this could be assured was to appoint Whig ministers, who would insist that this course be taken. Anne agreed, the Duke of Shrewsbury was made head of the government and the Protestant succession was saved.

On 1 August 1714 Queen Anne, the last of the Stuarts, died as the first of the House of Hanover was on his way from Germany to claim the throne.

The Stuart period was a century of great constitutional change. At the end of the Tudor period Queen Elizabeth was reigning as an absolute sovereign and Parliament was denied any real power. When the Stuart line came to an end with the death of Queen Anne, all this had changed. Parliament was now all-powerful and the divine right of kings was a principle in which only a few old-fashioned Jacobites still believed. The king now took a much less active part in the government of the country and it was the king's ministers who became responsible for the success or failure of the king's government.

The formation of the 'Cabal' ministry in the time of Charles II had led to a small cabinet of senior ministers who decided the policy of government, and it is to the Revolution that we owe government by party, the cabinet being chosen from the Party with the majority in the House of Commons.

Although the Commons of the early eighteenth century differed greatly from the Commons we know today, particularly in election and representation, it was the model on which it was built.

Finally, the greatest constitutional change was the union of England and Scotland and the creation of the Parliament of the United Kingdom.

The Stuart period must also be associated with the

number of literary figures who lived and wrote during that time.

Milton wrote *Lycidas* and *Paradise Lost*, Shakespeare, who died in 1616, wrote *The Tempest*, *Macbeth* and *King Lear* during James I's reign, and Bacon published *The Proficience and Advancement of Learning* in 1605 and his other works during the reigns of James I and Charles I.

John Bunyan, the author of *The Pilgrim's Progress*, was born in 1628, and Samuel Pepys kept his 'Diary' from 1660–1669.

During the latter half of the Stuart period, the poets included Lovelace, Dryden and Herrick, essayists Addison and Jonathan Swift, and Daniel Defoe wrote *Robinson Crusoe*.

Neither must we forget Sir Isaac Newton (1642–1727), who early in his life showed his amazing powers as a mathematician and thinker and discovered the law of gravity, and that most famous of architects, Sir Christopher Wren who designed many great buildings including St Paul's Cathedral. Inside this cathedral is a Latin inscription over one of the doors describing how Wren lies buried within its walls. It ends with the words: 'If you ask where is his monument, look around you.' No more fitting epitaph could have been placed over his grave. Wren and Newton were both leading members of the Royal Society that was formed in 1645 to encourage the study of the sciences.

Finally, there is one other name that must be recorded. William Harvey (1578–1657) deserves his fame for his discovery of the circulation of blood in the body that resulted in major advances in the arts of medicine and surgery over the ensuing years.

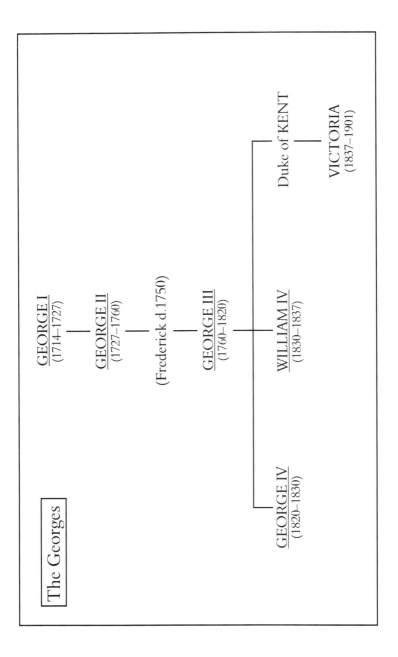

The Georges

GEORGE I
(1714–1727)
|
GEORGE II
(1727–1760)
|
(Frederick d.1750)
|
GEORGE III
(1760–1820)
|
GEORGE IV   WILLIAM IV   Duke of KENT
(1820–1830)   (1830–1837) |
                                        VICTORIA
                                        (1837–1901)

VI

The Georges (1714–1837)

i George I (1714–1727)

The true heir to the throne was the Catholic James Stuart, son of James II, and, but for the Act of Succession passed in 1707, he would have been declared king as of right. It was therefore by Act of Parliament that George, Elector of Hanover, became king. (Elector was the title given to the German Prince, being entitled to vote on the election of the Emperor.) But there were still many Jacobites who wanted to see the Stuarts back on the throne and from the beginning of his reign George was faced with serious dangers.

When George finally arrived in England he was welcomed by the Whigs, who had secured him the crown, but there was little general enthusiasm for him. He was old, unattractive and spoke no English, in direct contrast to the young and handsome Pretender. Nevertheless, if the people of England disliked a Hanoverian king, they liked a Stuart king even less and the reigns of Charles II and James II were still fresh in their minds. During the reign of Queen Anne trade had been prospering and a class of wealthy merchants had arisen who firmly believed that the return of the Stuarts would mean disaster for their trades and who therefore provided much-needed support for the new king.

For a short time there was peace at home and abroad but it did not last long. The Whigs who had brought over King

George were now in power and, when they decided to impeach members of the old Tory ministry, riots broke out in many parts of the country. So serious did they become that it was necessary to pass the Riot Act in order to put them down. The Act forbade twelve or more persons 'to unlawfully assemble to the disturbance of the peace' and provided for them to disperse within one hour if ordered to do so by the sheriff. Hence the expression 'read the Riot Act'.

Two of the most active Tory leaders, Bolingbroke and the Duke of Ormond, fled to the continent and joined James Stuart, the Pretender, to promote his cause for the crown. But it was at this time, 1715, that the old French king, Louis XIV, died and the Jacobites lost their strongest supporter. Nevertheless, James prepared to return to Scotland where he hoped to find strong support. The most powerful of Scottish highlanders was the Duke of Argyle, head of the Campbell clan, but the fact that he had taken the side of the Hanoverian king was enough to range most of the other Highlanders against him. In August 1715, the standard of the Pretender was raised at Braemar and a small army marched south. But the expedition was a failure: many of the highlanders refused to cross the Border into England and the English Jacobites were reluctant to join an enterprise which appeared ill-managed and badly led.

The rebels were finally defeated at Preston and retired to Scotland where the struggle continued with the Duke of Argyle. In January 1716 James landed at Peterhead only to find little support for his cause, and within a month he returned to France. Thus ended the rebellion known in England's history as 'The Fifteen'.

For the remaining eleven years of George's reign England was in constant dispute with the different powers of Europe. It must not be forgotten that George I was not only King of England but Elector (Prince) of the German state of Hanover. At this time Germany was divided into many different states which included Austria, the electorates of Bavaria and Prussia, and dozens of other principalities, both large and small. There was no union among them and they engaged in endless rivalries between themselves and the other countries of Europe, arranging alliances and counter-alliances, the parties constantly shifting sides. England found itself drawn into this political bear garden because King George gave priority to the interests of Hanover and the Catholic powers of France and Spain still supported the Stuart claims to the crown of England. But there was a further reason which drew our country into these European conflicts. England was becoming a major trading nation and, year by year, its ships were sailing further and further across the seas in search of commercial opportunities. This brought them into conflict with other European powers who had already seized possessions in such places as America, India and Africa. Although these powers were ready to fight to keep their colonial possessions, their priority was always to strengthen or enlarge their own borders at home. England on the other hand, being an island, had no opportunity to extend its own boundaries and therefore could direct all its resources towards building up its possessions abroad. When the long struggle was over, the boundaries of the European states had changed, some growing stronger at the expense of others who had grown weak, while Britain had gained an empire by acquiring massive possessions in every part of the world.

George I's reign will always be associated with the 'South Sea Bubble', because nothing that happened in those years excited more interest and concern to a great number of people.

England was by now heavily in debt. Since the time of William and Mary, when Charles Montague had first introduced the concept of a national debt, it had become a common practice to borrow large sums of money for the nation with the authority of Parliament. This was done principally in two ways. First, at a fixed rate of interest until repayment. The total sum borrowed in this way from all sources was known as the 'Consolidated Debt' and each lender was said to be a holder of 'Consols'. Second, the government raised funds on 'life annuities'. These sums were never to be repaid but a fixed rate of interest was guaranteed for the life of the provider. The interest paid on life annuities was high and, of course, the longer the recipient lived, the better the bargain he obtained.

At a time when it was not easy to save money safely and when there were few banks, investing in annuities became very popular and by the early eighteenth century a large number of people had done so. This set the scene for the disaster of the South Sea Bubble.

By 1720 the National Debt had become very large and the government was anxious to reduce it. A company known as the 'South Sea Company' was formed which was prepared to take over the National Debt. The agreement was that the company would pay off the debt owed to those who held annuities in return for generous government financial support in building up its business in the South Seas. The company then offered to repay the holders of the annuities, not in money but in shares in the company. It was strongly believed that the company, with government support, would be highly successful and the shares become very valuable. So, not only did the majority of annuity holders accept this offer but thousands of others sought to buy the shares. The price of the shares immediately started to rise and the eagerness to buy was so great that in a short time the shares went up to ten times their real value. The rich and the poor all fought to invest until the shares in the company and its subsidiaries were worth on paper five hundred million pounds, twice the then value of all the land in England. The bubble was bound to burst and burst it did. When it became clear that the shares had little actual value everyone tried to sell and the shares became virtually worthless. Thousands were ruined overnight and so great was the suffering throughout the country that Parliament was compelled to step in and help some of those who had lost everything they possessed.

The South Sea scheme had always been opposed by Robert Walpole on whom the king was coming to rely more and more and whose influence increased as each year went by. He was a man of peace and it is largely due to him that England avoided war during the last few years of George's reign. On 14 June 1727 George I died in Germany. He is not a very notable figure in England's history but his reign is not without importance. Speaking no English and caring more about Hanover than he did about England he took no active part in the government of country; he left that to his Whig protectors who held the majority in the Commons, their leader being granted the chairmanship of his council. It marked the beginning of a prime minister presiding over a cabinet, empowered to take all major decisions.

ii George II (1727–1760)

George II was undistinguished in every way but he had one advantage over his father – he could speak English. His reign was to last thirty-three years, during which events of great importance took place, although the part he played in them was of little significance as he relied almost completely on his chief minister to run the affairs of the country. His reign can be divided into two periods: the first a period of peace under Walpole and the second a period of war under Pitt.

Robert Walpole was prime minister for twenty-one years. He was a plain, stout man with a reputation for coarse manners and so eagerly did he seek power that he tended to get rid of those with the greatest ability, out of fear that they might rival his authority. For this reason he made many enemies. By now, of course, government by party was the rule in England and therefore the prime minister required the support of the majority in Parliament. This Walpole obtained by bribing Members of Parliament; this was a practice common at the time, although Walpole carried it out to a greater extent than it had ever been done before. But, having said that, Walpole was a wise man who thought the best policy was peace and who always acted in the best interests of his country rather than himself.

In 1737 when Queen Caroline, George's wife, died, Walpole lost a good friend who had frequently influenced the king on his behalf. But he had not only lost a friend; he had also found an enemy in her son, Frederick, Prince of Wales. He was a worthless young man who had quarrelled with his father and he soon became the centre of a party that was opposed to Walpole and his policies of peace.

After the death of the queen, this party felt strong enough to make an open attack on the Prime Minister, declaring that his efforts for peace had allowed the interests of the country to suffer, particularly abroad. Spain, it was said, had insulted and attacked British traders and the story of Jenkins' Ear was seized upon. Jenkins was a sea captain who alleged that he had been captured by the Spaniards in South America and had an ear cut off, which he subsequently carried around in a box. There were some who declared that Jenkins was a rogue who had had his ear cut off in the pillory, but whatever the truth of the story, it served its purpose. The cry was all for war and Walpole, much against his will, at last gave way, and war was declared against Spain in 1739.

Three years later he retired from the government, bringing to an end the political life of England's great 'Peace Minister' who had been the first to reside at 10 Downing Street. The scene was now set for the arrival of the great

'War Minister', William Pitt, who had joined the opposition Party of the Prince of Wales and was already rising to fame.

One of the only naval successes of the war with Spain was the capture of Portobello in Panama by Admiral Vernon, who used to wear a boat cloak made of a coarse wool stiffened with resin gum. This material was called grogram, so Vernon's sailors called him Old Grogram. When the admiral ordered the sailors' traditional tot of rum to be watered down, the rum ration thereafter became known as 'grog'.

It was also at this time that the song 'Rule, Britannia!'' was first heard, which was destined to become the one of the most famous British songs. James Thompson had written a masque about the father of the navy, Alfred the Great, which was entitled 'Alfred', and the opening lines were:

> When Britain first at heav'n's command,
> Arose from out the azure main
> This was the charter of the land,
> And guardian angels sang this strain:
> Rule, Britannia! Britannia, rule the waves;
> Britons never shall be slaves.

Note that it is not 'Britannia rules the waves', the way it is usually sung at the Proms in the Albert Hall. It was not a statement, but a command from heaven that Britain must rule. It was a declaration that Protestant Britons were chosen by heaven to rule.

The Spanish war of 1739 was the beginning of a long series of wars that lasted, almost without pause, for seventy-six years until 1815. The history of all this fighting is rather bewildering but there are one or two factors that stand out quite clearly.

Firstly, whatever happened and whoever were the

warring parties, England and France were sure to find themselves on opposite sides.

Secondly, the rise of Prussia. In 1740 'Frederick the Great Elector' ascended the throne of Prussia, determined to make his kingdom the chief among the German states (a position then held by Austria under the famous Empress Maria Theresa) and the following year a fierce war broke out between them.

Thirdly, while the fortunes of England in Europe varied greatly, the power of Britain overseas and particularly on the American Continent and India grew steadily from year to year while that of her great rivals, France and Spain, grew less and less.

The war that broke out between Prussia and Austria in 1741 saw England siding with Austria, and France with Prussia. On 27 June 1743 a battle was fought at Dettingen in Germany between the British and Austrians against the French. It resulted in victory for the British and their allies and is notable particularly because this was the last occasion when a reigning English king, George II, personally took part in a battle.

Now that France was openly at war with England the French planned to weaken their enemy by once more supporting a Stuart claim to the throne. James Stuart, the 'Old Pretender', was too old for further adventures but his son Charles, known as the 'Young Pretender', was more than ready to strike a blow to win back the crown. In 1745, escorted by a small French naval squadron, Charles landed in Invernesshire on 25 July and called upon the highlanders to help him. In some respects he had an advantage over his father because he was young, handsome, brave and likeable: 'Charlie is my darling, the young chevalier' runs a well-known Scottish song. Many of the highlanders were prepared to support him and so the 'Forty-Five Rebellion' got under way.

An army of 3,000 men under General Cope marched to

Edinburgh to quell the rising but were unable to resist the fierce highlanders and were defeated at the battle of Prestonpans. Charles then crossed the border and advanced as far south as Derby without any serious opposition. There was panic in London and the king actually prepared to leave the country because it was widely believed that, should the Pretender reach London, a French invasion would immediately follow.

It was at this time that the words of a patriotic song began to be sung in London to raise the spirits of the people. This was 'God Save the King', which was to become the national anthem in the following century.

But the people of London need not have feared. At Derby Charles' followers seemed to lose heart as there appeared to be no help coming from France, and Dutch troops were said to be on their way to support King George. The Scots turned and made their way back home and never again was an invading army to make its way on to English soil. Charles managed to rally his followers in Scotland and to defeat the royal troops at Falkirk, but on 16 April 1746 the rebels were heavily defeated at the battle of Culloden.

Charles managed to escape from the battlefield and was hunted throughout the country with a high price on his head. A young lady called Flora MacDonald disguised him as her maid in women's clothes and he finally escaped in a boat to Skye and thence back to France. His escape has forever been immortalised in the song:

> Speed bonny boat like a bird on the wing,
> 'Onwards' the sailors cry.
> Carry the lad who was born to be King
> Over the sea to Skye.

Culloden was the last battle to be fought on British soil and ended forever any chance of a Stuart restoration. The House of Hanover was secure.

In the wars on the continent and abroad there had been gains and losses on both sides with little overall profit to any of the nations involved and in 1748 the Treaty of Aix-la-Chapelle was signed. Unfortunately, the peace was not to last for long.

In 1746 the prime minister was Henry Pelham but the most active minister and one of the most powerful was William Pitt. When Pelham died in 1754, his brother the Duke of Newcastle became prime minister, but he was a man of little judgement or ability and between him and Pitt a fierce enmity arose. Pitt was determined that Britain's growing interests abroad should be protected. War with France had been threatening and local fighting had broken out in both America and India.

In 1756 the French sent an expedition to attack the island of Minorca in the Mediterranean which had been in British hands for forty years. Admiral Byng was sent with a small fleet to raise the siege, but when he arrived he decided he was so outnumbered by the French ships that they had little chance of success and withdrew without firing a shot. After a brave resistance the garrison of Minorca was forced to surrender. When Byng returned to England the fury of the people knew no bounds and a scapegoat was needed. The admiral was tried by court martial, sentenced to death and shot by a firing squad of Marines on board *HMS Monarch*.

In his play *Candide,* the French writer Voltaire derided the English for their treatment of Byng by writing that in England 'it is considered a good idea to put an Admiral to death every now and then in order to encourage the others'. The phrase *pour encourager les autres* is the origin of what has become a common expression.

By that time, 1756, Pitt's opposition to Newcastle had

became so extreme that he was driven from office and Pitt became prime minister, while war with France broke out again not only on the continent of Europe but also in America and India.

The story of the rise of British power in India and how the power of France was broken is the story of Robert Clive. In the same way the growth of the two states of America and Canada is the story of General Wolfe and George Washington.

We must look at each of these stories in turn because they recount how the foundations of the British Empire were built.

CLIVE OF INDIA

The Mogul Emperors in Delhi had for generations ruled over the greater part of India. But in 1739 the Mogul Empire was overthrown and various princes and chiefs entered into fierce struggles for their right to rule India. Such was the position when twenty-one-year-old Robert Clive arrived in Madras to start work as a clerk in the East India Company. Although he was a descendant of one of Cromwell's most famous generals no-one would have guessed he was to become a British military genius and a name for ever to be remembered in England's history.

The East India Company had received its charter in 1600 and by this time was still little more than a successful trading concern. The local native rulers allowed it to carry on its trade in a number of settlements, the principal ones being in Bombay, Calcutta and Madras. The French were also trading in India and at that time were in a stronger position than the British. Their chief settlement was at Pondicherry, south of Madras.

Both countries now suddenly appreciated that India was there for the taking and that a small trained European force, particularly with local native support, could easily impose their authority. Dupleix, the French governor, immediately took advantage of the opportunity by making use of the quarrels between the various native states, and a struggle for power with the British quickly developed. At first the French gained the upper hand, Madras was taken and a British attack on Pondicherry failed.

It was at this moment in 1746 that Clive first arrived on the scene. He hated his office work and longed to be a soldier, so he volunteered his services as an unpaid captain and from that day became the soul of the British party in India.

When peace was made between England and France in 1748 (the Treaty of Aix-la-Chapelle), there was no peace between the two countries in India and the tide of victory gradually turned in favour of the British. In 1751 Clive, with a tiny force, captured the town of Arcot and held it through a seven-week siege. The name of the defender of Arcot became famous throughout India and the legend of his invincibility was born. Again and again over the next two years he turned defeat into victory by his military skills and bravery.

In 1756 the terrible tragedy of the 'Black Hole of Calcutta' took place. Surajah Dowlah, the Nawab (or native ruler) of Bengal, attacked and captured the British settlement of Calcutta. Most of the inmates escaped by sea but 146 persons were left behind. They were imprisoned in the height of summer in one small room in which they could barely stand and by the following day only twenty-three were still alive. Clive vowed revenge and the next year that revenge was taken at the battle of Plassey.

On 23 January 1757 he headed a small force of 950 Europeans and 2,300 natives against an army of 68,000 men under Surajah Dowlah. The battle took place near Calcutta and resulted in an amazing victory for Clive who broke up and dispersed the enemy for the loss of only twenty-three men, helped by the desertion of a large number of the enemy soldiers. This victory added to the fame of Clive both in India and Great Britain and made the British masters of the three chief provinces of Bengal, Behar and Orissa. The influence of the British was thus extended throughout the native states while that of the French was all but destroyed. The foundations of the British Raj had been created.

In 1766 Clive achieved another notable victory but this time of a very different kind. In that year the British officers of the native regiments in the company's service, being discontented with their pay, mutinied. The Indian Mutiny posed a moment of great danger but was personally dealt with by Clive visiting the regiments, refusing to listen to threats and by his firmness and personality defusing the situation.

In 1761 Clive had been rewarded with an Irish peerage and returned to India three years later as Commander-in-Chief and Governor of Bengal. In 1767 he left India for the last time. The remaining few years of his life were not happy because he was bitterly attacked by those who had been offended by his imperialistic acts in India, and he was eventually driven to suicide in 1774.

AMERICA AND CANADA

In the West, as in the East, it seemed that the power of France was to prevail over that of England and the position of the British colonies in America was in jeopardy. At that time the North American continent stretched from the Arctic Circle to the Gulf of Mexico and the English colonists had mostly settled along the eastern seaboard, New England and in Canada. The French, on the other hand, held large territories in the south and in Canada in the Valley of St Lawrence, including the city of Quebec. The fear was that they would link their northern and southern possessions behind the back of the English settlers, shutting them off from the vast undeveloped areas to the west.

Pitt decided that a great effort was needed to maintain and improve the position and a large fleet and army was sent across the Atlantic while the colonists were formed into regiments under British officers. One of these young officers, in command of troops in Virginia, was George Washington. For some time the campaign continued without material advantage to either side. Fort Duquesne was captured by Washington who renamed it Pittsburgh in honour of his prime minister. Pitt now sought a leader to do in the west what Clive had done in the east, and his attention was attracted by a particularly gallant officer, Colonel Wolfe, who was given a command.

The French army was commanded by General Montcalm who had the great advantage of holding the strong fortress of Quebec on the St Lawrence river. It was situated on a rocky hill over the river and appeared impregnable, but Wolfe decided to attack it. Above Quebec were some steep crags known as the Heights of Abraham and, being considered a sufficient form of defence in themselves, were not sufficiently well guarded. Under cover of night Wolfe moved his troops up the river and climbed the Heights in the dark. By morning his army was positioned over Quebec. The battle was long and fierce and Wolfe was wounded three times, and died as the battle was ending. When told that the enemy was giving way in all directions, he cried, 'God be praised, then I die happy.' Montcalm was also wounded and died the next day. Quebec surrendered and from that day British fortunes in North America steadily improved at the expense of the French. The first major step had been taken in the founding of the Dominion of Canada

In the meantime, Britain and her allies were being successful in Europe and other parts of the world. Victories over the French were achieved in West Africa, Guadeloupe in the West Indies and off the coast of Portugal, where Admiral Hawke destroyed the French fleet in a full gale. In Germany, a British and Hanoverian force defeated the French at Minden, and Fredrich the Great was successfully campaigning against Austria and Russia.

King George II died in October 1760. He had himself done little to serve his country but at least he deserved its gratitude for having given unfailing support to his great minister, William Pitt, who established Britain on the path to world power.

We cannot close the story of the reign of George II without making reference to a remarkable man who worked in the cause of peace and religion: John Wesley (1703–1791). Educated at Charterhouse, he became a clergyman of the Church of England and, with his friend George Whitefield, started a religious society known as the Methodists. Their preaching drew enormous congregations and the number of Methodists grew rapidly. On his death in 1791, the Methodists formally separated from the Church of England and it now constitutes one of the largest Protestant denominations worldwide, with more than thirty million members.

iii George III (1760–1820)

George III was the son of Frederick, Prince of Wales, who had died ten years before; he was therefore the grandson of George II. He had been brought up as an Englishman and was a very popular twenty-two-year-old when he became king. He was obstinate and not very bright but he was well meaning and determined to 'be king' in that he wanted to captain the ship and to have ministers who would do what he wanted.

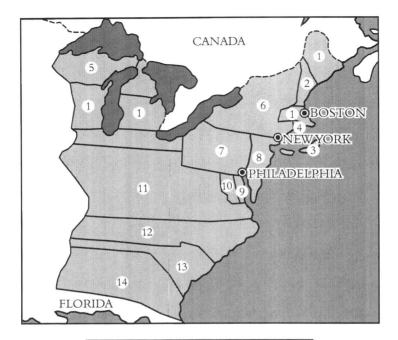

The United States (1783)

1. Massachusettes
2. New Hampshire
3. Rhode Island
4. Connecticut
5. N.W. Territory
6. New York
7. Pennsylvannia
8. New Jersey
9. Delaware
10. Maryland
11. Virginia
12. North Carolina
13. South Carolina
14. Georgia

Unfortunately what he wanted was nearly always the wrong thing to do.

In 1760 Pitt was still Minister but he resigned because he opposed the wish of Parliament to make peace with France, foreseeing that this could only lead to war with Spain. Lord Bute was then put in office to make the peace but, although a favourite of the king, he was incapable and disliked. War duly broke out with Spain (as Pitt had predicted) and peace did not come about until 1763, finally bringing an end to the seven years of war. Under the terms of the peace treaty of Paris, the islands of Martinique and St Lucia in the West Indies were given back to the French, but England kept the whole of Canada.

Shortly afterwards Pitt again became a member of government and in 1766 was made Prime Minister, being appointed to the House of Lords as Earl of Chatham.

A number of important events with far-reaching consequences took place during this long reign including the loss of the American colonies, the union with Ireland, the French Revolution, and Wellington's great battles with the French armies led by Napoleon Bonaparte culminating in the British victory at Waterloo in 1815.

It will probably be easier to follow these events if we deal with them separately.

THE AMERICAN COLONIES

In the reign of George II the greater part of North America had fallen into the hands of the British after the defeat of the French and, by the Treaty of Paris in 1763, England was allowed to keep the whole of Canada. British North America now became divided into two parts: Canada in the north remaining part of the British Empire, while the south became a separate country, the United States of America.

By this time the British in America had formed thirteen different colonies or 'states', the principal towns of which were New York, Boston and Philadelphia. These states were governed by Assemblies (or Parliaments) which had power to make laws but remained under the general jurisdiction of the British Parliament in London. In fact Parliament very seldom interfered and relations with the American colonies remained friendly until 1765 when steps were unwisely taken which heralded the end of this relationship.

Pitt had given up office and in that year George Grenville, the Prime Minister, introduced the Stamp Act. By this Act the American colonists were compelled to pay tax on legal documents and newspapers and it aroused strong opposition. When Pitt became Prime Minister as Earl of Chatham in 1766, this act was repealed, but he was unable to prevent a further act being passed that taxed tea, glass and paper imported into the American colonies and which was objected to as strongly as the Stamp Act had been. This resulted in riots and the Boston Tea Party, when colonists boarded merchant ships in Boston harbour and dumped their cargo of tea into the sea.

In 1770 Lord North became Prime Minister and he and the king became determined to make the colonists submit at any cost. The cost was the American War of Independence, which broke out in 1775 despite the vain efforts of Lord Chatham to avert this danger.

It began with the defeat of the British at Lexington after Paul Revere had spotted the British troops advancing in darkness and set off on his famous ride to warn the Patriots. George Washington was put in command of the colonists' army and on 4 July 1776 Congress, as the Colonial Parliament was called, passed Jefferson's famous Declaration of Independence which declared an independent nation, to be called the United States of America

Fighting continued with varying success on both sides. In 1777 the British were overwhelmed at Saratoga when an army of 3,500 men under General Burgoyne was forced to surrender, and a similar defeat was suffered by General Cornwallis at Yorktown on 19 October 1781. On this date Britain effectively lost its American colonies forever.

The war was now practically at an end although a peace treaty was not to be signed for another eighteen months. These were dark hours for Britain, which seemed to have enemies on every side, being at war with Spain, Holland, Sweden and France, the latter having actively assisted the American colonists with troops and ships. But 1782 saw two rays of light: Admiral Rodney destroyed the French fleet off Martinique and the three-year siege of Gibraltar by the French was finally raised.

In 1783 the Treaty of Paris formally ended the American War of Independence and George Washington became the first president of the United States. He was to prove himself as wise in peace as he had been skilful in war

THE RISE OF WILLIAM PITT

In 1783 Charles James Fox was leader of the government in the Commons under the Duke of Portland. He headed the Whig party and his power in the House was immense. The only person capable of opposing him was William Pitt, son of the great Earl of Chatham, who at the age of twenty-three Chancellor of the Exchequer and whom was quickly recognised as leader of the Tories. In public, Pitt was clever and resourceful, a brilliant orator with a commanding presence. In private he was a mixture of reserve and arrogance, a bachelor with few friends and indifferent to women.

The king was no lover of Fox, who had the support of the House of Commons, but Pitt had the support of both the king and the country. This led the king to dismiss Fox and make Pitt Prime Minister. It created a strange state of affairs: a prime minister of twenty-four with a majority of two to one against him in the House of Commons. Every measure he put forward was defeated, but Pitt would not give way because he knew the country was behind him. Parliament was dissolved in 1784 and at the ensuing election Pitt was sent back to office with a large majority. He was to be prime minister for the next seventeen years.

THE ACT OF UNION WITH IRELAND

In order to understand what happened in Ireland, we must go back in our history and recall what had taken place over the previous 300 years. Although the original conquest of Ireland began with Henry II in 1155, by the sixteenth century England had no real control beyond a small area around Dublin called the Pale. Beyond that area it was effectively bandit country and ungovernable, hence the expression 'Beyond the Pale'. It must be understood that although most of England had become Protestant after the Reformation, by far the larger part of Ireland had remained Catholic, although there were still a considerable number of Protestants in the north. Since the days of Elizabeth, and indeed before, there had therefore been almost continuous civil wars, which had caused great suffering. On several occasions English armies had been sent to Ireland to put down rebellion and, as we have seen, this happened in Cromwell's time and in the reign of William III when the Catholics, supported by the French, were defeated at the Battle of the Boyne. This had resulted in the Catholics being treated with great severity and left scars that were hard to heal. There was also a political reason for the Irish troubles. Since 1494, under Poyning's Law, the Irish Parliament could make no laws except by consent of the English government, but in 1782, just after the end of the American war, this law was repealed.

This was brought about by Henry Grattan, an eloquent Irish politician, who enrolled thousands of armed Irishmen called 'Volunteers', which encouraged Fox to give Grattan what he wanted: an independent Irish Parliament. Grattan's Parliament, as it was known, sat for the first time in 1782. However, all its members were Protestant, no Catholics were allowed to sit in it and disturbances continued to break out all over the country.

During the following years the Catholics united in an effort to compel the government to repeal the laws which prevented them from taking part in most areas of public life and from voting for Members of Parliament. In 1793 the Catholic Relief Act was finally passed, which gave them what they asked for. But this had little effect in ending the troubles and the divisions between the two religious camps remained.

In the end, Pitt made up his mind that the only way to resolve the situation was to treat Ireland as Scotland had been treated in 1707, by allowing the Irish to send members to Parliament in London instead of keeping a separate and independent Parliament in Dublin.

Accordingly, a bill was brought into the Irish House of Commons for the purpose of creating a Parliamentary Union and a similar bill was passed without difficulty in the British Parliament. In Ireland, however, there was fierce difference of opinion and one of the stumbling blocks was the English practice of buying and selling parliamentary seats whereby a rich person could 'own a seat'. Pitt was therefore forced to spend over a million pounds to buy out the 'owners' of such seats in order to get rid of a separate Irish Parliament. The Bill was finally passed on 18 February 1800 and became known as 'The Act of Union'. Since that day the Irish have been represented in England's House of Commons.

THE FRENCH REVOLUTION

For many years the government of France had been going from bad to worse. Government was in the hands of Louis

XVI and a few nobles who knew little and cared less about the sufferings of the majority of the country. A number of clever writers and speakers began to preach to the people that they should be free to rule themselves and that all men should be equal. This was a doctrine eagerly accepted by a discontented and oppressed people, who decided that the time had come to get rid of the king and government who had done them so much harm.

Thus began the French Revolution in the year 1789, a movement that spread like wildfire through the country. The cry was 'Liberty, Equality, Fraternity' and the Marseillaise, now the national anthem of France, became the song of the Revolution.

On 14 July 1789 the Bastille prison in Paris was attacked and destroyed. It held only a handful of prisoners but it represented the absolute rule of the monarch. The hatred that had festered for so long broke out against the nobles and the rich – the Aristocrats as they were called – and terrible scenes of massacre and bloodshed took place. The guillotine was set up in Paris and hundreds were publicly beheaded.

Louis XVI had married Marie Antoinette, the sister of the Emperor of Austria, and an Austrian army was sent to rescue her. The leaders of the Revolution called on all Frenchmen to fight against the Austrians and, unbelievably, an ill-provided and badly trained French rabble proved more than a match for the veterans of Austria and the invaders were defeated. On 17 January 1793 the National Convention, or Parliament of the Revolution, voted for the king's death and he was beheaded in front of a howling crowd. Later that year his beautiful queen followed him to the scaffold.

When the Revolution had started there was a body of opinion in England that supported it, and Fox himself welcomed the prospect of change. But by 1792 the French monarchy had been overthrown and mass murders of the aristocracy occurred daily. 'What had been anticipated as constitutional reform was turning into a bloody dictatorship and dictatorship was turning into war'.

Already at war with Austria, in February 1793 the revolutionaries declared war on Holland and Britain. It was a war that was to continue for twenty-two years with one short break and finally ended with the defeat of the French at the battle of Waterloo.

THE WAR WITH FRANCE (PART I)

Throughout this war the French armies were commanded by Napoleon Bonaparte, one of the most extraordinary men in modern history. A Corsican, he distinguished himself as a young colonel of artillery, was made a general and in 1796, at the age of twenty-seven, was given command of the French army against the Austrians.

The war began with a British naval success when Admiral Howe defeated a French fleet off Ushant on 1 June 1794, a victory made memorable as 'The Glorious First of June'. At this time Napoleon had not only beaten the Austrians but had compelled the Spaniards, as well as the Dutch, to side with France because he wanted the help of their fleets in order to take control of the seas from the British and invade Britain. He actually made preparations for this invasion but was thwarted by the destruction of the Spanish fleet off Cape St Vincent in 1797. It was in this battle that Horatio Nelson, a young captain of one of the British ships, displayed such skill and bravery that his fame originated from that day.

But the year 1797 also witnessed a very unfortunate episode in England's naval history. The treatment of sailors and the conditions in which they lived on board their ships was lamentable and had bred serious discontent. This came to a head when the crews of the ships at Spithead mutinied and refused to obey their officers. However, they maintained discipline and stated their grievances respectfully. Admiral Howe acted sensibly, made concessions, defused the situation and persuaded the men to return to their duties. But a far more serious mutiny also broke out at the Nore when ships were actually drawn across the mouth of the Thames to blockade London. Panic set in, but the government remained firm and the mutineers lost their nerve and gave in. Later that year the navy's reputation was restored with another naval victory, this time against the Dutch at Camperdown.

In 1798 Napoleon sailed with a French army to Egypt, hoping to conquer that country and open the way to India. The French army was landed and quickly overran Egypt but on 1 August Admiral Nelson discovered the French fleet drawn up at anchor close to the shore in the Bay of Aboukir. A bold night attack destroyed thirteen of seventeen ships, three of the others later being captured. It was an overwhelming victory that marooned the French army in Egypt. Nothing daunted, Napoleon led his troops northwards towards Constantinople on his planned route to India, but once again he was thwarted by a naval officer. The town of Acre was an obstacle in his way but a small Turkish garrison under Captain Sidney Smith defied all his efforts to take the city. At last relief came from the sea and Napoleon was forced to raise the siege and retreat, giving up all hope of conquests in the east and returning to France. Once back in France he soon took over the reins of power and was made 'First Consul', head of the government. It was a position he was to keep for the next fifteen years.

France now had a strong government and a strong army under Napoleon who then persuaded the northern powers, Russia, Sweden and Denmark, to join with France in refusing to allow British vessels to carry cargoes into their ports. This agreement was known as the 'Armed Neutrality' and caused great loss and economic suffering in England. Once again the British navy came to the rescue, being ordered to retaliate by seizing the cargoes of any ships going to or from the ports of France or her allies.

In the meantime Pitt, in his efforts against the French, was being hampered by weak and untrustworthy members of his own party and was continually attacked by Fox. Finally the quarrels within his party became so bitter that in 1801 Pitt was forced to resign, having been driven to a low physical and mental ebb and probably already suffering from the cancer that was later to end his life.

Within a month of Pitt's resignation the navy won another famous victory, this time against the Danes at the battle of Copenhagen. The British fleet was commanded by Sir Hyde Parker and under him was Admiral Nelson who led the attacking ships. There was overwhelming firepower from the Danish positions which caused severe damage to the British ships and Admiral Parker signalled for Nelson to discontinue the action. Nelson, who had previously lost his right eye (and arm) in battle, clapped his telescope to his blind eye and declared: 'I really do not see the signal'. He continued the attack and, although heavy losses were sustained, in the end the victory was decisive. It is from this incident that the expression to 'turn a blind eye' is attributed.

In the same year the Emperor of Russia was murdered and his successor Alexander I at once made peace with England. Later that year arrangements for a general peace were put in hand, although there were those who did not believe that any peace would last or that Napoleon could be trusted. However, he consented to the terms which were arranged at Amiens on 27 March 1802.

The Peace of Amiens lasted less than a year. Those who had not trusted Napoleon were correct in their judgement because he used this respite to prepare for a second and more successful war. Relations during the peace quickly disintegrated and when Napoleon openly insulted the British Ambassador in Paris, war broke out again. Feelings between England and France became even more bitter when Napoleon imprisoned all the English who happened to be in France at that time. In May 1804, when the French made obvious preparations to invade England, Pitt, for the last time, was persuaded to return as Prime Minister. In the same year Napoleon assumed the title of Emperor and thereafter reigned as the absolute monarch of France.

It was a time when Britain needed a strong hand at the helm. Thousands of French soldiers were gathering in a great camp at Boulogne and were being trained in boats for the invasion. Pamphlets were printed in English, ready to be distributed to the people of Britain, telling them that they were being freed from the tyranny of their government in exchange for the benefits of the great French Revolution. Everything was soon ready for the invasion except one thing: the invading army was on the wrong side of the Channel and the British navy had control of the sea. Napoleon knew he had either to destroy the British fleet or to have it out of the way at the time of the invasion.

As the ships went into action Nelson hoisted on his flagship, the *Victory*, the famous signal: 'England expects that every man will do his duty.' Every man did his duty and by nightfall nearly the whole of the enemy fleet had been captured or destroyed. But sadly Nelson, struck down by a bullet fired from the masthead of the French ship *Redoubtable*, died in the hour of victory. The whole nation was plunged into grief and news of the great victory seemed little compensation for the loss of their beloved protector.

Lemuel Francis Abbot, Horatio Nelson, 1797, National Portrait Gallery, London.

Although the power of France on the seas had been finally broken and Britannia now truly ruled the waves, they had lost their hero.

The danger of the French invasion vanished with the victory at Trafalgar and no one knew this better than Napoleon. He therefore removed his army from Boulogne marched to Austria and overwhelmingly defeated the Austrian army at the battle of Austerlitz, which made him virtually master of Europe.

A month later, on 3 January 1806, when all Pitt's efforts to support and strengthen England's allies seemed to have failed, he succumbed to his illness and died. He was forty-seven and had been a member of the government for half that time. There was no one of his character and ability to replace him. His great political enemy, Fox, took office as Foreign Secretary under Lord Grenville, but within eight months he too was dead. They were buried close together in Westminster Abbey, which provoked Scott to write a well-known poem, the last lines of which read:

> The solemn echo seems to cry –
> Here let their discord with them die.

THE WAR WITH FRANCE (PART II)

It was now clear to all the world that Napoleon aimed at nothing less than the conquest of the whole continent of Europe to be followed by the conquest of Britain. England had become the poorer for the loss of three great men: Nelson, Pitt and Fox. But it was not long before another star was to appear on the horizon, possibly the brightest of them all: Arthur Wellesley, later Duke of Wellington.

In 1807 a new ministry was formed after Fox's death, of which the principle members were Lords Castlereagh and Canning, who quickly became implacable enemies. Castlereagh was a highly capable political leader but became widely unpopular and was held in contempt by England's liberals for the repressive measures he took following the end of the Napoleonic wars. In 1810 the king, whose sanity had long been in question, was deemed permanently insane and George, Prince of Wales, became Prince Regent.

In the meantime, in 1806 France picked a quarrel with

Prussia, destroyed her army at Jena and occupied Berlin. Russia, alarmed at this sudden defeat of the king of Prussia, sent an army to his aid but they were again defeated at the terrible battle of Eylau the following year. France now seemed invincible, but one power, Britain, still remained unconquered and unconquerable.

While France was extending her boundaries in Europe, Britain was adding to her Empire overseas. British power in India had been steadily growing. 1803 saw the routing of a huge native army by General Wellesley at the battle of Assaye, while in the same year General Lake captured Delhi and Agra. 'The Gate of India', the Cape of Good Hope, having been given up at the Treaty of Amiens, was captured a second time and the colony of British Guyana was wrested from the Dutch.

Napoleon now realised that he could not destroy the naval power of Britain on the sea, so he determined to destroy it from the land. In November 1806 the Berlin Decree was issued declaring the British Isles to be blockaded, all commerce forbidden and all British vessels refused admission to any port in France. In this way Napoleon hoped to bring Britain to its knees by destroying the enormous trade carried out by British ships. However it soon became clear that, although Napoleon's scheme succeeded to some degree, so dependent was the continent itself on British imports, he was in fact inflicting even greater suffering on France and its European allies and the plan failed.

Now that the shores of Britain had been shown to be safe from the French, the British government decided the time had come to take on France in Europe and troops were sent to Spain. Thus began the Peninsular War in 1808. Spain was already under the power of France where Napoleon's brother, Joseph, had been made king and in 1808 the French invaded Portugal and took possession of

Lisbon. It was at this stage that a small force under Wellesley, recently recalled from India, landed in Portugal and, to the astonishment of all Europe, defeated the French veterans at Vimiera and by the Convention of Cintra forced them to abandon Portugal.

A second British expedition was then sent to Spain under Sir John Moore to assist the Spanish armies that were still resisting French rule. When news arrived that the Emperor himself was advancing at the head of the powerful army, the Spaniards everywhere gave way and Moore's small army was forced to retreat to Corunna on the north-west coast of Spain. Once again the British navy came to the rescue but not before a ferocious battle in which Sir John Moore was mortally wounded.

From that day forward the reinforced British troops in Spain were more successful and the French were to be gradually driven back into their own country. In 1809 Austria again declared war on France and again suffered defeat, Napoleon once more marching in triumph to Vienna where he compelled the Emperor of Austria to give him his daughter, Marie Louise, in marriage. That same year Arthur Wellesley defeated the French for the second time in Spain at the battle of Talavera and was rewarded with the title of Viscount Wellington. But neither side was able to gain full advantage: the French were still too strong and England's Portuguese and Spanish allies too weak for Napoleon to be forced out of Spain. Two years later, in May 1811, another bloody but indecisive battle was fought at Albuera, but in 1812 Wellington received some important news. The peace between France and Russia was at an end and the Emperor had decided to embark on one more great war to strike at the heart of Russia. Troops could therefore no longer be spared to support Joseph Bonaparte in Spain and the end of the French dominance of Spain was in sight.

On 24 June 1812 the Emperor's Grand Army of 450,000

men crossed the river Niemen into Russia. In September, after a terrible battle at Borodino in which 80,000 were killed and wounded, they entered Moscow only to find the city deserted. The next day great fires broke out all over the city which had been started by the Russians, who preferred to see their city destroyed rather than occupied by the French. Winter set in, provisions ran out and Napoleon had no choice other than to retreat – but retreat in the heart of a Russian winter meant death. Cold and famine took its dreadful toll and scarcely 20,000 returned to cross the frontier into the safety of France. It was a disaster to be replicated by the retreat from Russia of the German army in the winter of 1941/42.

In the meantime, Wellington was driving the French out of Spain. Two strong fortresses which blocked the road to France were finally stormed and captured and in June 1813 the French army was routed at Vittoria. King Joseph Bonaparte fled from Madrid and by the following spring the French were finally defeated on their own territory, under the walls of Toulouse. Austria and Prussia now joined forces with the Russians and on 16 October 1813 their combined armies forced the Emperor to do battle outside Leipzig in Saxony. Nearly half a million men were engaged in this battle which ended in a crushing defeat of the French. Six months later, on 4 April 1814, Napoleon agreed to abdicate and was sent to the little island of Elba off the Italian coast.

The brother of the beheaded Louis XVI was made king of France as Louis XVIII, the Bourbons had returned to the throne and peace had at last been restored to Europe. But not for long – there was to be one last confrontation with the French.

In March 1815 Napoleon escaped from Elba and landed at Cannes in the South of France. His old soldiers rallied to his support and within a few days he was in Paris with a

French army that had sprung up as if by magic. He immediately launched attacks on British troops at Quatre-Bras. They were unprepared and retired to Waterloo, a small town near Brussels, which became the stage for probably the most famous battle of them all. The battle lasted for only one day: 18 June. It raged fiercely all morning, the French making charge after charge, and the loss of life was terrible. When the result was in the balance, a Prussian army under General Blucher arrived in early evening and the day was famously won.

Napoleon escaped to Paris where he gave himself up and was confined on the little island of St Helena in the South Atlantic. He died there in May 1821 and the British government allowed his body to be returned to Paris where he was buried with great pomp under the dome of the 'Invalides'. Thus ended the life of the 'greatest Frenchman of them all' who for so long had been the most feared man in Europe.

When George III died in 1820, the sixty years of his reign had seen Britain emerge as the most powerful nation in the world. Canada, Australia (where Captain Cook had raised the union jack at Botany Bay in 1770) and most of India were only a part of the British Empire and Britain dominated international trade. But at home it was a period of unrest among the 'working class' which represented a huge majority of the seven million population. Economic reform was long overdue, unemployment was rife and rising due to the discharge of 300,000 servicemen after Waterloo, and the condition of the poor was steadily deteriorating. Revolution was in the air when 80,000 people attended a meeting in St Peter's Fields in Manchester to be addressed by 'orator' Hunt, one of the extremist leaders. The local yeomanry were unable to arrest him, so the magistrates sent in the Hussars and in the panic hundreds received sabre wounds and eleven were killed. It became known as the 'Peterloo

Massacre' and caused further repressive measures to be instituted. Such was the situation when George IV ascended the throne.

iv George IV (1820–1830); William IV (1830–1837)

Old King George III died in 1820, blind, insane and unlamented. He was succeeded by his son, the deplorable George IV, who had been an ineffectual Prince Regent for the last nine years. It was once more a time of peace, the only conquests being those of science and invention and the reform of the political system. It has been said that the history of 'modern' England begins after the year 1815.

Castlereagh committed suicide in 1822 by slitting his throat, overcome by the paranoia which developed as a result of his unpopularity and an abortive attempt on his life. Lord Byron, one of his liberal foes, penned this dreadful epitaph:

> Posterity will ne'er survey
> A nobler grave than this.
> Here lie the bones of Castlereagh
> Stop, traveller, and piss.

He was followed as Prime Minister by Canning, and in 1828 by Wellington with Robert Peel as Home Secretary. Although Wellington was opposed to Catholic emancipation (the right of Catholics to sit in Parliament), in 1829 the Catholic Emancipation Act was passed to avoid facing the possibility of civil war in Ireland.

In 1830 George IV died and was succeeded by his brother, William IV. In the same year Wellington's ministry came to an end over his refusal to agree to Lord Grey's plan for a Reform Bill and Lord Grey became Prime Minister to head the first Whig government for sixty years. This resulted in the Reform Bill, which increased the categories of persons who had the right to vote, being finally passed in 1832.

Two other famous names served in this Whig Ministry, Lord Melbourne and Lord Palmerston, both future prime ministers, and no time was lost in carrying out other important reforms.

The slave trade had been abolished in 1807 and now the work of Wilberforce was completed in the year of his death by an act that set free all slaves belonging to British subjects anywhere in the Dominions. Further, an effective Factory Act was passed limiting the hours worked by children, prohibiting their employment under the age of nine and, importantly, appointing inspectors to see that these provisions were enforced.

In 1834 Gray resigned as Prime Minister to make way for Lord Melbourne, who was at the height of his political influence when William IV died in 1837 and Victoria came to the throne.

v   The Arts in The Eighteenth Century

The Georgians ruled for over one hundred years (1720–1837) and it was a period rich in literary and artistic talent. In this nutshell it is possible to do no more than list some of the principal names and works.

Samuel Johnson wrote his *English Dictionary* and *Lives of the Poets* and was himself immortalised by his friend Boswell in *Boswell's Life of Johnson*.

Oliver Goldsmith was made famous by his book, *The Vicar of Wakefield* and his play *She Stoops to Conquer*; Grey composed the much-quoted poem 'Elegy in a Country Churchyard' and in 1749 Henry Fielding published his novel, *Tom Jones*.

Famous artists of this century included Hogarth, Turner,

Gainsborough, Constable and Joshua Reynolds who became the first president of the Royal Academy, which was opened in 1769.

William Cowper wrote his poems and ballads, Sheridan his *Rivals* and *School for Scandal* and Lamb his *Tales from Shakespeare*.

Byron, Shelley and Keats were among the best-known poets, together with the Scotsman Robert Burns and the 'Lake Poets' – Southey, Wordsworth and Coleridge – who lived and wrote in the Lake District of Cumberland. Sir Walter Scott wrote his stirring poems and that great tale of chivalry, *Ivanhoe*.

It was truly a century of immense achievement in the arts, not to mention, in other fields: Watt's steam engine, Arkwright's spinning jenny and the opening of the first railway from Manchester to Liverpool when Stevenson's Rocket drew its train at 30 mph. We should also note that in 1789 the Marylebone Cricket Club, the MCC, celebrated its second birthday and Thomas Lord established the famous ground where the game is still played.

VII

Queen Victoria (1837–1901)

i   The Early Years (1837–1861)

In June 1837 William IV died. He left no children and the next heir to the throne was his niece Princess Victoria, daughter of his younger brother. She was just eighteen when she was crowned in great splendour and two years later she married her cousin, Prince Albert of Saxe-Coberg. He was not the most educated prince in Europe but was a talented man of intelligence and for the next twenty years, until his death in 1861, he became the queen's closest advisor, helping to set the standards for Victoria's popular and successful reign, which lasted over sixty years. It was a reign that saw many changes and improvements in the lifestyles of nearly all sections of society throughout the country and the further extension and consolidation of Britain's empire overseas. So much happened during the Victorian era that it is only possible in this concise history to refer to those principal events and reforms that had the most profound effects.

Victoria ascended the throne at an unhappy time in England when the first signs of a great economic depression were appearing. Lord Melbourne headed the Whig government and immediately devoted himself to teaching the young queen her royal and constitutional duties, lessons she was never to forget. But the people had lost faith in his party. Working conditions in the factories were appalling, wages were minimal, the Poor Laws inhuman, and it was at

Sir George Hayter, Queen Victoria, 1838, National Portrait Gallery, London.

Francis Xavier Winterhalter, Prince Albert of Saxe–Coburg-Gotha, 1867, National Portrait Gallery, London.

this time that Dickens' protest against workhouses, *Oliver Twist*, was first published. It was therefore not surprising that there was a clamour for political reform as a means of addressing these wrongs and the so-called Chartists came into being. A charter was drawn up listing all the required political changes including votes for all men by ballot, and a monster petition was prepared which a huge crowd tried to bring before Parliament. But Parliament refused to receive any claim supported by violence and force, and this led to serious rioting in various parts of the country, the worst being in Newport, where soldiers fired on the crowds. Although the Chartist leaders were imprisoned or transported, these events led to the social, commercial and political changes that were to take place over the next fifty years.

It was in 1838 that a movement first began against the laws by which imported corn was taxed. All imported goods were taxed, but the duties on corn were designed to support the price of home-grown wheat, which pleased the landowners, although many others suffered from the enforced high price of bread. Melbourne supported the Anti-Corn Law League but failed to persuade Parliament to remedy the situation and as a result he resigned in 1841. Robert Peel then became prime minister at the head of the new Tory Conservative party. Although he originally opposed the abolition of the Corn Tax, he now appreciated that the economic situation desperately required the repeal of the Corn Laws which, after two failed harvests, was being demanded by the distressed people of England who were literally starving in some parts of the country. But the Conservative party was split on this major issue, the Protectionists being forcefully led by a young man called Benjamin Disraeli, son of a Spanish Jew who had been an MP for only a few years. However, on 25 June 1846 a bill was forced through Parliament and the Corn Laws were repealed, cutting all import tariffs on grain to a peppercorn sum. It was a great victory for Peel and crowned his life's work, but within days he was forced to resign over the problems in Ireland.

In 1846 Ireland was nearly destitute due to a grain famine. Four million people were living almost entirely on potatoes when in the spring of that year the potato crop failed and Ireland faced disaster. Peel acted immediately and sought emergency powers through a Coercion Act. It was a bill that deserved to receive full support from both sides of the House, but Disraeli and his friends saw an opportunity to get their revenge on Peel and voted against it. Peel lost by a few votes and resigned, and four years later in 1850 he was killed in a riding accident in Green Park.

Not only had Robert Peel been ultimately responsible for the abolition of the duties on corn, but by removing or reducing many other duties he took a long step towards promoting Free Trade, in the course of which he split the Tory party into Free Traders and Protectionists. He will also be remembered for first introducing income tax (which has remained with us ever since), a Mines Act, which stopped females and boys under ten from working underground, and setting up the original London police force whose officers are still referred to as 'bobbies'.

When Peel resigned the Tories were too split among themselves to form the next government and the Whigs under Lord John Russell, with Palmerston as his Foreign Secretary, once again took over. They enjoyed twenty years of almost uninterrupted power, but it was destined to be the last Whig government in England's political history because a new political group was about to emerge. The Liberals, a mixture of Peelites, Whigs and other politically homeless radicals, were to become one of the two major parties of the next sixty years.

Lord John's Whig government survived for six years,

during which a Ten Hours Act was passed limiting the working hours of children and females in factories. The Public Health Act of 1848 made provisions for cleaner water, proper drainage, refuse collections and better housing conditions. The penny post had been started and in the next twenty-five years the numbers of letters posted increased from 50 million to over 650 million. Gas light, Christmas cards, photography and the first telegraph lines were introduced by the middle of the nineteenth century and a network of railways was spreading all over the country. Abroad, Hong Kong had been ceded by the Chinese, Malta had been annexed, the Cape of Good Hope taken, and Sir Thomas Raffles had bought Singapore. By 1851 when the Great Exhibition was opened in Hyde Park there was therefore good cause for celebration and the nineteen-acre Crystal Palace was considered the structural marvel of the century.

In 1852 Lord John Russell's government collapsed and was followed by the Earl of Aberdeen heading the first ever coalition government. 1854 saw the start of the Crimean War when Great Britain, together with France, joined Turkey in its war against Russia in order to protect British interests in the Mediterranean and the route to India. The story of this war, which lasted nearly two years, is one of mismanagement, suffering and loss. Lord Raglan was commander of the British forces. He was sixty-six, a fairly undistinguished general who gave his name to the raglan sleeve because of the style of his coat. The cavalry was led by Lord Cardigan who likewise had his woollen jacket, the cardigan, named after him. In September 1854 the allied armies landed on the Crimea Peninsula in the Black Sea, won the first battle on the river Alma and laid siege to the town of Sebastopol, which was to last eleven months. At Balaclava the heroic blunder of the charge of the Light Brigade took place when 600 men were blasted to death by the Russian fire, and shortly afterwards many more were killed at the battle of Inkerman.

Meanwhile the terrible Russian winter closed in on the army in front of Sebastopol, rendering the losses in battle minimal compared with those from cold, starvation and disease. At the end of 1855 the Russians were at last forced to surrender and in March 1856 this unnecessary war was brought to an end, the total loss of life being estimated in excess of one million.

It was a conflict which settled nothing and the only real victory was that of Florence Nightingale who, by her devotion to the wounded and skills of organisation, saved hundreds of lives and will ever be hailed as the saint of that disastrous war.

The mismanagement in Crimea proved the downfall of Aberdeen's coalition government and Palmerston, at the age of seventy-one, at last became prime minister, rapidly becoming a favourite of the queen. He ended the Crimean War by negotiating the Treaty of Paris, but was almost immediately faced with another major crisis in another part of the world, the Indian Mutiny.

The two Sikh Wars had been fought between 1845 and 1849 as a result of which the Province of the Punjab and other parts of India were added to the British possessions in that vast country. Thereafter the Sikhs became the most loyal subjects of the queen and fought with distinction for her on many occasions. But now, in 1857, the dangerous Indian Mutiny broke out, threatening the authority of the British in India, which at that time was still being administered by the East India Company. This was a mutiny among the Sepoy (or Hindu) regiments of that Company and had clearly been plotted for a long time, although the catalyst was the provision of cartridges, which were believed to be greased with cow's fat, to the Indian troops. To Hindus the cow was a sacred animal which could not be killed or eaten and at that time it was necessary to bite off the top of the cartridge before loading, which would bring the soldiers' lips into contact with the fat. It seems likely this was an excuse rather than the cause of the mutiny which initially broke out in Meerut and soon spread to all parts of India as other regiments murdered their officers and marched on Delhi. The next few months became a saga of human suffering and death as small British garrisons defended themselves with great bravery against overwhelming numbers. Cawnpore held out for twenty-one days and, when forced to surrender, all the men, women and children were massacred in cold blood and thrown down a well. At Lucknow a few British and loyal native troops held out in the Residency and were finally relieved after 141 days of immense hardship. Troops were hurried from England to assist and after Delhi was retaken on 20 September 1857 the fate of the mutineers was sealed, their regiments were destroyed or disbanded and their leaders put to death. By the end of 1858 the British government had regained its power throughout the country and British rule was once more firmly established.

It was then decided that the government of a country as large as India could no longer be left in the hands of a private company such as the East India Company and that it should come under the authority of the queen and her Ministers. As a result, on 1 November 1858 Queen Victoria was proclaimed 'Sovereign of India' and head of its government.

1861 saw the beginning of the American Civil War between the north and the south. The slave-owning southern states wanted to break away from the union with the north and the overall authority of President Abraham Lincoln, but the government and the people of the northern states would not allow this and were prepared to fight to preserve the united status. The north, who were in favour of abolishing slavery, won the day after a bitter

Queen Victoria as Empress of India, 1877, Hulton Archive

struggle lasting nearly five years. Unfortunately almost the whole of England's cotton imports came from the southern states of Alabama and Tennessee and, because the north blockaded all the ports in the South, those imports ceased to arrive while the war lasted. This was a disaster for the English cotton mills and the 600,000 workers who depended for their livelihoods on the cotton industry, because this Cotton Famine led to mass unemployment and left many destitute. Only when the war ended were the mills able to reopen and the cotton industry revived.

1861 was a most unhappy year for Queen Victoria. In March her mother, the Duchess of Kent, died with Victoria at her bedside and for the next six months the queen struggled with her grief. At the end of the year she was therefore ill-prepared for the death of her husband from typhoid at the age of forty-two. She went into the deepest mourning, grew thin and weak and almost certainly suffered a serious nervous breakdown, some even fearing for her sanity. She never fully recovered from her grief and built the elaborate Albert Memorial in Kensington Gardens in eternal memory of the man she loved and upon whom she had placed so much reliance.

ii   The Later Years (1862–1901)

The early 1860s saw Bismarck, President of Prussia, take giant strides towards establishing Germany as the major power in Europe. In 1864 Prussia seized the duchies of Schleswig and Holstein from Denmark while Palmerston stood by, despite the fact that Britain had a treaty with Denmark and the previous year Bertie, Prince of Wales, had married Princess Alexandra of that country. Within a year Prussia had also routed Austria and thereafter Germany's relentless pursuit for power in Europe led to the two world wars in the first half of the twentieth century. By now

Palmerston was over eighty and although he won the General Election of 1865, within a few months he was dead. Lord Russell again became Prime Minister, to be followed almost immediately by Lord Derby, with Disraeli as Chancellor of the Exchequer and Leader of the House. This parliament is best remembered for the Second Reform Bill, which for the first time gave the vote to the urban working class man who was a householder, but not to those in the rural areas. This was designed by Disraeli to gain the support of the working class for the Conservatives, but he apparently failed because they lost the following year's election by a large majority and Gladstone then formed the first Liberal Government.

This great ministry saw the banning of the transportation of criminals to the colonies, the founding of the TUC., the simplifying of the judicial system, and the overhaul of the army. The Ballot Act (1872) allowed votes to be secret and the Education Act (1870) provided extra schools and local school boards, thereby establishing a foundation for a national system of education which a few years later became compulsory and free. Gladstone also tackled the problems in Ireland, where there was growing agitation for an independent Irish Republic. He managed to force through the Irish Church Act after a battle in the Conservative House of Lords which disestablished the Protestant Church in Ireland and rid a Catholic nation of its hated Protestant dominance.

Despite the successes of this first Liberal government, in 1874 the Conservatives returned to majority government for the first time for nearly thirty years and Disraeli, now over seventy, seized his chance to at last become Prime Minister, the queen sending him to the Lords as the first Earl of Beaconsfield. Although Disraeli was a champion of the working classes and set about to improve matters such as social welfare, slum clearance and public health, his principal interest was to promote British power and interests abroad by enlarging and strengthening the Empire. In 1869 the Suez Canal had been opened providing a shorter route to India and the Far East, which, together with the advent of the steamship, transformed Britain's global strategic position. In 1875 Disraeli arranged the purchase of Suez Canal shares from the bankrupt Khedive of Egypt for £4 million, giving Great Britain a majority shareholding and control of this vital new route to the east. Britain and France also took over financial and administrative control of Egypt. In addition, control of the eastern Mediterranean was secured when Turkey ceded the island of Cyprus to Britain in gratitude for Disraeli's help in negotiating favourable peace terms with the Russians.

Nevertheless, when the next election came in 1880 Gladstone and the Liberals were back in office and within months Disraeli was dead, bringing to an end the remarkable career of an extraordinary statesman. That same year the Boers of the Transvaal rose in rebellion. These Dutch settlers had moved en masse from the Cape area fifty years before ('The Great Trek'), disillusioned by British imperialism and the passing of a law freeing all slaves, and had settled in the Transvaal. After diamonds were discovered in that country and Britain declared the land round the mines to be their territory, the Boers took up arms, inflicted a crushing defeat on the British army at Majuba Hill and the Transvaal was given up to them.

A major crisis then developed in Egypt. The Egyptian army rose against the French and British administration in their country and, after this uprising had been subdued, control of the Sudan was seized by a fanatical religious leader known as 'Mahdi'. General Gordon was dispatched to withdraw the small and scattered native garrisons serving under British officers, but the general himself was trapped in Khartoum and Gladstone's delay in sending troops for his relief resulted in his death. The British people were outraged and Gladstone was never forgiven.

Closer to home, the government was once again faced with serious problems in Ireland. The plight of the Irish farmers was as acute as ever and the Irish Land League, headed by Charles Parnell, had become very active in campaigning for compensation for the thousands of evicted tenants. When a Bill to provide such compensation was thrown out by the Lords, Irish fury knew no bounds and led to serious violence by extremist groups (including the Fenian Society, who were the forerunners of the IRA) and the murder of the Chief Secretary in Dublin. Parnell preached the peaceful tactic of ostracising those who took advantage of eviction. Captain Boycott was the name of one such person and he remains for ever condemned after his name became an accepted word in the English language. Home rule was another major focus for agitation and Gladstone finally became convinced that it was necessary, although it turned out to be his downfall. A bill was introduced to give the Irish control of their internal affairs through a Parliament of their own, but it was defeated when many of Gladstone's own members voted against it. This resulted in the Liberal Party becoming irretrievably split and in 1886 the Conservatives found themselves back in power under Salisbury and were destined to remain so for the rest of Victoria's reign.

The last decade of Victoria's reign saw two further conflicts abroad. Thirteen years after the murder of General Gordon in Khartoum, his tragic death was avenged when Britain, having remained in occupation of Egypt, reconquered the Sudan under General Kitchener. But it was the Boer War in South Africa that cast a shadow over Victoria's last two years.

Sixty years before, thousands of Dutch settlers had taken part in the Great Trek from the Cape to free themselves from British rule and had settled in the Transvaal and

Orange Free State. After the Boer uprising in 1880–1881 ('Boer' is the Dutch word for farmer) relations with the British settlers, who arrived in large numbers seeking gold and diamonds, continued to worsen. Cecil Rhodes, who had gone to South Africa as a young man, had founded the diamond company De Beers and was now looking to mine the neighbouring territories of the Transvaal (which were subsequently named Rhodesia after him). The Boers saw themselves threatened and when Dr Jameson, the colonial administrator and friend of Rhodes, led a raid on the Transvaal which failed, relations with the British colonists (or 'Uitlanders') neared breaking point and the Boers began to arm themselves for war. It broke out in October 1899 when President Kruger declared the Transvaal Republic a sovereign international state.

England seriously underestimated the strength and fighting abilities of the Boers, who were more at home on the veldt than the British and whose farmer troops ('Commandos') were tough, knew the terrain and excelled at hit-and-run tactics. The British found themselves decisively beaten in three of the early battles and Kimberley, Ladysmith and Mafeking came under siege. But three divisions of reinforcements under Lord Roberts and General Kitchener were hurriedly provided and gradually the campaign turned in favour of the British. Within a year both the rebel capitals had been occupied but, although the war was effectively won, a fierce guerrilla campaign was carried out by the Boers for another eighteen months. Peace was finally signed in May 1902 when the two warring states were annexed to the British Crown and led to the Union of South Africa in 1910. One of the heroes of this war was Winston Churchill, who had been sent there as a special correspondent by a newspaper, the *Morning Post*. He was caught in an ambush, fought bravely, was captured and escaped after many adventures. He eventually returned home, stood as Conservative candidate for Oldham where he won the seat at the age of twenty-six and thus began his great parliamentary career.

The Victorian period was rich in the arts, with its abundance of talented writers, poets and painters. Dickens, Thackeray, the Brontë sisters and George Eliot (a pseudonym used by Marian Evans) were writing their famous novels, and the poets of that time included Wordsworth, Tennyson, Browning, Swinburne, Coleridge and Matthew Arnold. Others, such as Macaulay and Carlyle, and painters such as Turner, combined to create a period of incomparable artistic talent.

By the turn of the century Queen Victoria's health was failing. In January 1901 she was eighty-one years old and had been on the throne for sixty-three years, the longest reigning monarch in the history of England. That month she died at Osborne House on the Isle of Wight with her family at her bedside and the whole nation was plunged into mourning. The high standards of her private and public life, her devotion to her royal responsibilities and her strength of character changed the people's attitude to the throne. As Churchill said: 'She became the symbol of the British Empire.'

At her request she had a white funeral and was buried at Windsor alongside her devoted Albert, whose dressing gown she asked to be placed in her coffin.

And so ended the Victorian Age. By this time England was the most powerful, respected and prosperous nation in the world, but the next fifty years were to see that position change dramatically. By the 1960s, after two world wars, most of the British Empire had been relinquished, America had become the world's dominant nation, Russia posed the major threat to the stability of the western world and Britain's political and economic strength had sadly declined.

But the history of our country in the twentieth century is another story and it is a story to be told at another time.

List of Illustrations

King Henry VII, by an unknown Flemish artist. By courtesy of the Trustees of the National Portrait Gallery

King Henry VIII Painting after Holbein. By courtesy of the Trustees of the National Portrait Gallery.

Sir Walter Raleigh. Oil Painting by Hubert L. Smith. Oriel College, Oxford.

King Charles I. Triple portrait by Van Dyck. Reproduced by gracious permission of H.M. the Queen.

Blenheim Palace, from Colin Campbell, *Vitruvius Britannicus*, 1717.

Horatio Nelson, Viscount. Portrait by L.F. Abbot. By courtesy of the Trustees of the National Portrait Gallery.

Queen Victoria. Portrait by G. Hayter. By courtesy of the Trustees of the National Portrait Gallery.

Albert, Prince Consort. Portrait by F.X. Winterhalter. By courtesy of the Trustees of the National Portrait Gallery.

Queen Victoria as Empress of India, 1877. Photo *Radio Times* Hulton Picture Library.

Index

War of the Spanish Succession, 108
Warbeck, Perkin, 52
Warwick, Earl of
    'The Kingmaker', 45, 46
    See also Edward IV (nephew).
Washington, George, 125, 128, 132, 133
Watt, James, 149
Wellesley, Arthur. *See* Wellington, Duke of
Wellington, Duke of, 142, 144, 147
Wesley, John, 129
Westminster
    Abbey, 16, 31, 32, 34, 37, 142
    Hall, 21
    School, 77
Whigs, 104, 107, 110, 115, 148, 151, 155
Whitefield, George, 129

Wilberforce, William, 148
William I (William the Conqueror), 19–21
William II, 21–22
William III, 99, 103, 104–7
    See also national debt.
William of Normandy, 16
William of Orange. *See* William III
William Rufus. *See* William II
Wolfe, General, 125
Wolsey, Thomas, 57, 58, 59
Wordsworth, William, 165
Wren, Christopher, 98, 112
    See also St Paul's Cathedral.
Wyatt, Sir Thomas, 66
Wycliffe, John, 41, 43
    Lollards, 41
Yeomen of the Guard, 54
York, House of, 45, 46, 47, 48, 51

Made in the USA
Lexington, KY
23 May 2011